Self-Harm in Adolescence

Iva Burešová

Self-Harm in Adolescence

PL ACADEMIC RESEARCH

Bibliographic Information published by the Deutsche Nationalbibliothek
The Deutsche Nationalbibliothek lists this publication in the Deutsche Nationalbibliografie; detailed bibliographic data is available in the internet at http://dnb.d-nb.de.
Library of Congress Cataloging-in-Publication Data
Names: Burešová, Iva, 1972- author. | Hochmanová, Dita, translator.
Title: Self-harm in adolescence / Iva Burešová ; translation, Dita Hochmanová.
Other titles: Sebepoškozování v období adolescence v kontextuzivotního príbehu. English
Description: Frankfurt am Main ; New York : Peter Lang GmbH, 2016. | Translation of the author's thesis Sebeposkozování v období adolescence v kontextu zivotního príbehu (doctoral-Masaryk University, 2015). | Includes bibliographical references.
Identifiers: LCCN 2016017106 | ISBN 9783631667514
Subjects: | MESH: Self-Injurious Behavior--prevention & control | Adolescent
Classification: LCC RJ506.S44 | NLM WS 462 | DDC 616.85/8200835--dc23
LC record available at https://lccn.loc.gov/2016017106

The publication is released with the support of the Faculty of Arts at Masaryk University as a part of the following project: Internationalization of Publishing Support MU ROZV/20/FF/PU/2015. It draws on the results of specific research MUNI/A/0790/2011 and MUNI/A/0887/2012.
Translation: Dita Hochmanová
Language reviewer: Nelly Korec

ISBN 978-3-631-66751-4 (Print)
E-ISBN 978-3-653-06383-7 (E-Book)
DOI 10.3726/ 978-3-653-06383-7

PL Academic Research is an Imprint of Peter Lang GmbH.

Peter Lang – Frankfurt am Main · Bern · Bruxelles · New York · Oxford · Warszawa · Wien

This publication has been peer reviewed.

www.peterlang.com

Table of Contents

Introduction

In the last decades there has been a visible increase in self-harming behaviour in the non-clinical population of adolescents on the European as well as the world scale. In the most comprehensive European research study published so far, *Child & Adolescent Self-harm in Europe (CASE) Study*, which was conducted in 2000–2001 (Madge et al., 2008), the 11.1% prevalence of self-harm was found in a sample of 30477 adolescents. Subsequent studies then state even a considerably higher occurrence of this phenomenon – up to one fifth (Brunner et al., 2007; Swahn et al., 2012). Although this fact could have been influenced by the increased interest of specialists in researching this phenomenon and the related development and specification of adequate diagnostic tools, it is certain that this specific behaviour, until recently considered highly pathological, is becoming a norm in this key developmental stage to such an extent that a significant number of adolescent individuals try it at least once in their life or even practice it for an extended period of time.

Currently, we therefore cannot consider the concept of self-harm only in the context of psychiatric diagnoses, or disharmonic personality development, but it is necessary to perceive it as one of the important risk factors, which are commonly a part of the process of becoming physically and emotionally mature in the contemporary generation of adolescents. However, the great majority of self-harming adolescents never seek the help of a psychologist, psychiatrist, doctor or another adult person (Hrubá, Klimusová & Burešová, 2012; Hawton, Saunders & O'Connor, 2012). The available research findings do not answer the question of why these things are happening, nevertheless this alarming discovery makes it important to raise awareness of the occurrence, progress, possible causes, ways of treatment, and other crucial matters related to self-harm in professional and non-professional public. One of the reasons why this phenomenon is marginalised by the society is also the lack of understanding of the causes which lead adolescents to voluntary experience of physical pain.

1 Self-Harm Classification System Development

Self-harm seemingly appears to be a rather new phenomenon of the current age. However, the truth is that similarly to, for example, mental anorexia, its manifestations can be traced to the distant past[1], portrayed in a number of works of art and bibliographical references. The term self-harm itself was first used in the case study by L. E. Emerson *The Case of Miss A: a Preliminary Report of a Psychoanalytic Study and Treatment of a Case of Self-Mutilation* (Emerson, 1913). Emerson refers here to this behaviour as "self-mutilation", building his study on psychoanalytical basis and recognising self-cutting as a symbolic substitution of masturbation. Menninger (1935; 1938) is another important author in this context. He uses the same term in his studies and further distinguishes between suicidal and self-harming behaviour. However, he considers self-harm a partial suicide. In his view, this behaviour has a specific purpose and occurs under various circumstances and conditions. He defines it as a certain "weakened" wish to die and therefore introduces the term "partial suicide" into specialised literature (Menninger, 1935, p. 460). Menninger states 6 types of self-mutilation: 1) neurotic (biting nails, picking off scabs, excessive hair pulling out, unnecessary cosmetic procedures), 2) religious (self-whipping, etc.), 3) maturity ceremonies (circumcision, hymen removal), 4) psychotic (eyes, ears, genitals removal, extreme amputation), 5) based on organic damage (where repeated head banging and biting and breaking fingers occur, etc.) and 6) conventional (cutting nails and hair and shaving). Despite these first efforts to define and classify self-mutilation, relatively little attention has been paid to this behaviour by specialists until the late 70s of the 20th century (Yates, 2004). Specialised literature on this topic appeared very sporadically and to a great extent focused on self-harm only as on a symptom of some of the clinical diagnoses (e.g. personality disorder,

---

1 The history of mankind is full of references to self-harm. The Greek playwright, Sophocles, around 500 B.C. wrote a story of Oedipus, who gauged his eyes after realising the horrid fact that he had had a sexual intercourse with his own mother The Holy Bible contains a great number of references to self-torture. Vincent van Gogh cut off the lower part of his left ear with a razor in 1888. The poets of the 60s and the 70s of the 20th century wrote about self-harm without the intention of dying (Messer & Fremouw, 2008) and the works of contemporary artists portray it in full openness as a common part of coping with an inner crisis.

mental retardation, etc.).[2] However, in spite of this fact, we can still trace several important milestones, which formed the understanding of self-harm as a unique phenomenon throughout history.

In 1967, Graff & Mallin carried out a research study focused on self-harm, especially on wrist cutting, aiming to trace the causes of this behaviour. At that time, the impact of psychoanalytical theories had already decreased (Dominique & Roe-Sepowitz, 2005) and the influence of behaviourism was on the rise. Due to this influence, we can encounter new classifications of self-harm based on the description of the given behaviour. The above-mentioned authors described self-mutilation as follows: "In the past several years wrist slashers have become the new chronic patients in mental hospitals, replacing the schizophrenics" (Graff & Mallin, 1967, p. 74). In most respondents, the research found difficulties in communication and behaviour resulting from early deprivation. Self-harm was also the subject of the study titled *The Syndrome of Delicate Self-Cutting* by Pao in 1969, where he distinguished between self-harming individuals who harm themselves in a delicate way (delicate) and those who harm themselves in a rather coarse way (coarse). In his opinion, in the first group of individuals one cannot assume a suicidal aim. However, he noted this behaviour as relatively repetitive. In the second group of individuals, he observed the usual suicidal aim, which can even result in death. The author finds that the "delicate cutters" were usually young people who suffered from multiple attacks of self-harming surface cutting and were often diagnosed as suffering from a borderline personality disorder. In contrast, "coarse cutters" were usually older and often psychotic.

At the turn of the 70s and 80s, Ross & McKay (1979) introduced their classification of self-harm and highlighted the necessity to distinguish between direct self-harm (cutting, biting, excessive rubbing, cutting off parts, inserting objects, burning, swallowing or inhaling, hitting oneself and strangling) and indirect self-harm (overeating, drug abuse, etc.). Subsequently, Pattison & Kahan (1983) described in their work the typical characteristics of intentional self-harm – repetition, long-term nature, low mortality, and the intention to harm oneself – and suggested that intentional self-harm should be distinguished as a unique diagnostic syndrome. The authors also distinguished three basic elements of self-harm – the so called "self-harming acts" – which are: *directness or indirectness of self-harming behaviour* (referring to whether the behaviour is caused by a direct or indirect intention to mutilate oneself – some of the indirect acts are e.g. smoking, alcoholism, or not following medical treatment), *frequency of repeating* (the act can be one-time or repeated)

2 Self-harm was actually viewed this way until the recent past.

and *high or low mortality* (among the acts with high mortality is a suicidal attempt, or a suicide). By combining these elements, eight additional groups were created, which the authors used to classify all forms of self-harming behaviour from smoking to premature ending of treatment of serious illnesses or even to suicide.

In 1987, the ground-breaking monograph *Bodies under Siege: Self-Mutilation in Culture and Psychiatry* by Armando Favazza is published. Favazza, in his work, uses the term "self-mutilation" and distinguishes between culturally accepted self-mutilation (e.g. piercing) and deviant self-mutilation, which he further classifies. Despite various gradual changes in his original conception that the author made throughout his lifetime research, he always strictly separated self-harm from suicidal behaviour and highlighted different motivation behind both acts. He was drawing on an assumption proven by practice that an individual who attempts suicide wants to end his or her life, while a person who intentionally harms oneself has the opposite aim – to feel better. In his study from 1990, he proposes a new taxonomy system of self-harm (Favazza & Rosenthal, 1990), which is used and respected to this day.

Another, very clear, classification system appears in the publication by Welshe and Rosen (1988), *Self-Mutilation: Theory, Research and Treatment*. Based on their research in specialised literature, its authors postulate and support Favazza's innovative thought that self-harming behaviour should be strictly separated from suicidal attempts and both phenomena should be understood as separate clinical units in clinical practice. In their classification, the authors use four degrees, which they define by the level of physical mutilation, mental state of the individual, and the extent of social acceptance of the given behaviour. Intentional self-harm, as understood by the majority of authors, should be closest to the third type in their classification system.

Table 1. Classification system by Walsh and Rosen (1988)

TYPE	BEHAVIOUR EXAMPLE	DEGREE OF PH. DAMAGE	MENTAL STATE	SOCIAL ACCEPTANCE
I.	piercing, tattooing…	surface to mild	positive, harmless	acceptance in most social groups
II.	ritual scaring…	mild to moderate	disturbing	acceptance in specific subcultures
III.	cutting wrists and the body, burning with a cigarette…	mild to moderate	mental crisis	generally socially unacceptable behaviour
IV.	autoamputation, autocastration…	serious	psychotic decompensation	totally unacceptable behaviour

Later on, Favazza and Simeon revised their taxonomical system of self-harm and laid the basis for currently its most frequently used division. In the last and most up-to-date version of their classification, they distinguished four categories of self-harming behaviour and considered the first three categories pathological: *Stereotypical self-mutilation*[3], which typically occurs in individuals with pervasive developmental disorders and other illnesses (e.g. autism, mental retardation, etc.) – such behaviour does not consider social context (e.g. the presence of onlookers), does not have affective content and it is repeated and rhythmical; *Serious self-mutilation*, which includes serious mutilation of the body (e.g. auto-castration or gauging one's eyes) resulting in permanent damage and often occurs as a unique event in the course of a psychotic attack; *Compulsive self-mutilation*, manifested by repeated or ritual behaviour, which often occurs several times per day (e.g. pulling out hair, biting nails, scratching)[4]; and *Impulsive self-mutilation*, defined as direct, socially unacceptable damage of tissue, which occurs without the intention of killing oneself and without pervasive developmental illness or psychosis. Such behaviour can be rare or repeated – when rare, it includes individual episodes of self-mutilation (e.g. cutting, burning, hitting oneself), which are usually caused by the preceding feeling of tension and after the act of self-mutilation the tension reduces and the person feels better. Isolated incidents can grow with time and the particular behaviour can gradually turn into an addiction (Simeon & Favazza, 2001)[5].

Unfortunately, all the subsequent classification systems significantly lack unified terminology, which is caused mainly by the fact that for some authors, self-harming behaviour includes manifestations of behaviour with the intention to

---

3 In clinical symptoms, this behaviour can have the form of stereotypical self-harm, which is usually repeated monotonously, sometimes even rhythmically. Mostly, it has the form of hitting oneself in the head or other parts of one's body, biting oneself, pulling out one's teeth, dislocating one's joints, etc. It can appear in mentally retarded or autistic people. However, it can also be connected with acute psychosis, schizophrenia, Lesch-Nyhan syndrome, Cornelie de Lang syndrome, Rett and Tourett syndrome.

4 Current psychiatric taxonomy diagnostically classifies it as an impulsive disorder (e.g. trichotillomania).

5 This classification is significant because it distinguishes the category of impulsive self-mutilation (it distinguishes this category from stereotypical self-mutilation), serious self-mutilation (which occurs in psychotic people) and compulsive self-mutilation (which is a symptom of other possible psychiatric diagnoses). When most of the current studies mention self-mutilation, they are talking about Favazza's impulsive self-mutilation. It is the first big step to distinguish self-harm as a separate phenomenon as opposed to 'mere' symptom of other mental illnesses.

die behind it. Moreover, very often the unity of terminology by various authors does not mean the unity of content[6].

Favazza's work broadened awareness of self-mutilation by including not only professional but also non-professional audience. Subsequently, this type of behaviour was considerably publicised in media by personal testimonies of celebrities, like Angelina Jolie and Lady Diana Frances Spencer, etc. Following their example, a number of teenagers admitted such behaviour (Messer & Fremouw, 2008) and self-harm gradually gained the attention of psychologists, doctors, pedagogues specialising in the education of children with behavioural disorders and broader professional and non-professional public. The last important milestone in the development of classification of professional public attitude to self-harm was the year 2013 when the term Non-Suicidal Self-Injury was introduced into the American Psychological Association Manual DSM-V™ (see chap. 2.2.).

1.1 Definition of Terms

Despite the preliminary establishing of self-harm as an isolated symptom in the diagnostic manual DSM-V™, we cannot find its unified and generally acknowledged definition in relevant specialised literature because it is a complex phenomenon and its exact description entails a number of disunities in terms of terminology resulting from the various ways of understanding it. Therefore, in specialised literature, we can find various terms for self-harm, which very often have more or less the same meaning. The most common terms are: Self-Harm, Self-Injury, Self-Mutilation, Parasuicide, Self-Battery, Deliberate Self Harm (DSH), Local Self-Destruction, Self-Cutting, Focal Suicide, Self-Inflicted Violence, Delicate Cutting, Self-Abuse, Self-Injurious Thoughts and Behaviour and other. Using these terms in research and clinical practice is very often given by particular region. The terms Self-Harm and Deliberate Self-Harm are used especially in Great Britain, whereas the terms Self-Injury, Self-Mutilation, Self-Inflicted Violence and Self-Injurious Behaviours are used rather in the USA (Suttno, 2005).

Very frequent terms, which are used especially in research studies, are Non-Suicidal Self-Injury (NSSI) (Brausch, Gutierrez, 2010) and Repetitive Self-Mutilation

6 E.g. the term "Deliberate Self-Harm" is understood by Tantam a Whittaker (1992) in their study as the most general term for the type of behaviour that entails the intention to harm one's body, and which therefore also includes a suicidal attempt. In contrast, Sutton (1994) does not include the type of behaviour directly aiming to end one's life under this term.

Syndrome (RSM). Leiberman (2004) states that this term includes activities which can be identified as self-injurious behaviour, parasuicidal behaviour and deliberate self-harm. Based on the form of self-harm, more specified terms, like Symbolic Wounding, Slashing, Scaring and other, appear.

The frequency of using various terms and changeability of their content meaning can also be observed in the historical context, which shows the progress in perceiving self-harm: from a type of behaviour closely connected with suicidal behaviour (Kreitman, 1977) to realising the importance of mechanisms through which self-harm actually prevents suicide (Ross & McKay, 1979; Simpson, 1975; 1980 and others) to perceiving self-harm as a type of behaviour which completely lacks suicidal motivation.

Currently, the umbrella term Self-Destructive Behaviour is being used in a number of studies for self-harming behaviour (see Sutton, 2005; Duffy, 2006). It covers all the types of behaviour which lead to deliberate self-harm with any level of lethality. This term includes previously used labels, like Self-Mutilation (auto-mutilation or self-mutilation), Self-Harm, Self-Battery, Deliberate Self-Harm (one-time or periodical behaviour with direct intention to physically harm oneself but without the intention to die, deliberate self-harm, self-injury), suicidal behaviour most often denoted by the term Suicide, Parasuicide (suicidal attempt), Attempted Suicide, which is connected with direct intention to die or with the expression of the intention to end one's life. However, this term also newly includes Risk-Taking (which is a term for long-term behaviour without a direct intention to harm oneself or die – it includes smoking, alcohol and drug abuse, performing risky sport activities, etc.) and it also acknowledges the categories of Self-Poisoning/Overdosing and Self-Injury.

In its broadest meaning, the term Self-Destructive Behaviour can therefore cover any injury aimed against oneself. In this context, Sutton uses the term Self-Inflicted Violence (2005). Under this perspective, the spectrum of activities, which could be included under the term Self-Destructive Behaviour, is broad. On the one side of this spectrum, there would be phenomena as frequent in today's society as, for example, drinking alcohol or smoking cigarettes, restriction in food intake or, on the other hand, overeating, excessive amount of exercise and even broadly culturally accepted body decorating in the form of various types of piercing and tattoos or even less accepted creating of decorative scars (so called scaring). Although these body-modifying techniques are not generally understood as deliberate self-harm because of their primarily decorative character, some writers put them in this category[7]. On the other side of the spectrum of activities which are seen as self-destructive, we can find very rare extreme behaviour, which includes significant and coarse injury of body tissue[8] occurring in some psychiatric patients in connection with acute psychotic states[9], or suicide.

Despite its inconsistency, the currently used terminology most often takes into account the criterion of a certain level of directness of this behaviour and the seriousness of the damage consequently caused, or the aforementioned level of lethality. Another traditionally stated differing criterion is repetition of such behaviour. In spite of certain differences, we can therefore find the same elements in a number of currently used definitions of self-harm, which unfortunately does not prevent the contents of the terms from overlapping. Nevertheless, most writers describing this behaviour agree on its basic components: an individual performs the acts on himself/herself, deliberately and with a purpose in mind, at various levels of physical violence. However, according to most authors, this behaviour is not suicidal and does not include sexual or decorative intention.

One of the most popular and most frequent definitions in specialised literature is the following: "Self-mutilation (SM) refers to the deliberate, direct destruction or alternation of body tissue without conscious suicidal intent" (Favazza, 1998, p. 259). Many more authors (e.g. Ross & Heath, 2002) use this definition as the basis for their own research. Hawton & Harris (2007) define "Deliberate Self-Harm" as an act with non-fatal consequences in the form of behaviour causing damage (cutting oneself, jumping from high places), use of a drug which exceeds the prescribed limit, eating non-edible matter or an object, or taking illegal or recreational drugs with the intention to harm oneself. Skegg (2005) describes Self-Harm as a broad scale of behaviour and intentions including attempted hanging, surface self-cutting or impulsive self-poisoning carried out in response to an unmanageable burden. In foreign literature, the most frequent definitions describe self-harm in the meaning of a deliberate act of destructing of one's own tissue with the aim of shifting unbearable emotional pain to physical pain, which is more manageable for the individual (Janis and Knock, 2008; Hicks and Hinck, 2008 and others). These authors claim that in an extreme interpretation of self-harm, it can be defined as a visual demonstration of extreme

7 Laye-Gindhu &Schornert-Reichl (2005) observes more frequent occurrence of tattoos in people who mutilate themselves.

8 It might be, for example, an eye enucleation, castration or limb amputation.

9 Most often it is an acute psychotic episode, schizophrenia, mania, serious depression, or acute intoxication.

emotional anxiety and in their writing we can encounter the broadening term "Self-Injurious Thoughts and Behaviour".

More recent surveys and comparative studies (see Ougrin et al., 2012) use the term "Self-Harm" relatively broadly, regardless of the intention of such behaviour. In Great Britain and Europe, suicidal attempts are also often included under this term. In contrast, in the US it is much more common to distinguish self-harming behaviour based on its intention, and thus the term Non-Suicidal Self-Injury (NSSI) is more frequently used here. According to Lloyd et al. (2007), NSSI is perceived as intentional behaviour which results in mutilation or alternation of body tissue without a conscious suicidal intention. With regard to the aim of this publication and the above-mentioned facts, the term Self-Harm will be used primarily from now on.

1.2 Differentiation from Suicidal Behaviour

In recent years, the research in the area of self-harm repeatedly highlighted the necessity to specify the theoretical paradigm of self-harm, which would, among other things, also contribute to its more precise differentiation from suicidal behaviour (Jacobson et al., 2008). In the newest issue of DSM-5, Non-Suicidal Self Injury has been detached as a separate chapter in the part called Conditions for Further Study (DSM-V™, 2013). This chapter includes areas which seem to be crucial for the clinical sphere. However, currently there is not enough data to include them among individual mental disorders[10]. At the same time, the chapter suggests criteria for independent diagnosis of NSSI (In-Albon et al., 2013a), but along with the suggested diagnostic category they are a subject of further inquiry at the moment (In-Albon et al., 2013b), despite the fact that their content is in

10 A major sign of NSSI is repeated creating of small but painful wounds on the surface of one's body. The most frequent cause of such behaviour is the effort to get rid of negative emotions, like tension, fear, or self-hate and/or solve an interpersonal problem. In some cases the behaviour is understood as a deserved punishment. Individuals often talk about an immediate feeling of relief, which occurs during the act of self-harm. If the behaviour occurs regularly, it is often accompanied by the feeling of urge and desire, in its character similar to addiction. Self-inflicted wounds can be deeper and more frequent with time. The wounds are most often knife or razor blade wounds, needle sticks or sharp injuries. The usual places of self-inflicted injuries are the front part of thighs and the dorsal part of forearm. Other methods include stabbing (most often into the upper arm) with a needle or a sharp knife, burning by a cigarette, "burning" of skin by repeated rubbing with an eraser. Using more than one method is associated with more serious psychopathology, including suicidal attempts." (DMS-5, 2013, p. 803–804).

accordance with the definition of NSSI commonly used in American research studies. Nevertheless, specialised literature more and more often highlights the need to diagnostically anchor self-harm in an appropriate way, not only for research purposes but also for the needs of common clinical practice. According to Nock (2012), it is necessary to work on its clear definition as well as on the correct use of given specialised terms in this context.

The level of lethality and motivations closely related to it has become one of the main diagnostic criteria for categorisation of self-harm as a separate clinical category. This helps distinguish such behaviour from suicidal attempts and suicidal behaviour (Hawton & Rodham, 2006). With regard to the frequency of its occurrence and even possible lethal consequences, it is necessary to pay increased attention to suicidal behaviour in this sensitive developmental stage[11]. Unfortunately, a number of research studies still examine suicidal attempts and self-harm together. Some of them use these terms inaccurately and then identify a suicidal attempt with self-harm (Wong, Brower & Zucker, 2011) – especially because a suicidal attempt is often difficult to identify (Claes & Vandereycken, 2007). However, a suicidal attempt is significantly different from self-harm in many ways, according to the results of a number of conducted research studies (Pattison & Kahan, 1983; Sabo et al., 1995; Motz, 2001; Brown, Comtois, & Linehan, 2002 and others), and it is different in more than one category. A suicidal attempt is based on the intention to die and it is different in its aetiology, function of the behaviour, and also its frequency. This behaviour also differs from self-harm in the age when the first episode occurs. While suicidal behaviour hardly ever occurs before the age of 15, in case of self-harm this age limit is usually lower – around 12 years of age and it can occur in younger individuals as well (Bertolote & Fleischmann, 2002). Moreover, current definitions of self-harm (see above) mostly deny that any intention to die is directly related to this behaviour, which is also supported by a number of research claims (Brown, Comtois, & Linehan, 2002 and others).

Most of the research conducted in this area also highlights the fact that self-harming behaviour brings the feeling of release. The moderation of inner pain, on the contrary, prevents suicidal tendencies (Liberman, 2004). Great majority of

11 According to Patton (2012), in the Western world, suicide is the second most frequent cause of death after accidents on the roads – in female adolescents aged 15–19 yrs. it is the most frequent cause of death and in male adolescents the third most frequent cause of death (after accidents on the roads and violence). Current research confirms that suicide is becoming an important cause of death in adolescents even in developing countries (Ougrin et al., 2012).

individuals who harmed themselves state tension release, not ending their lives, as their primary aim. Therefore, it is possible to say that self-harm can be closely related to suicidal tendencies, but not directly or causatively. Also, according to Sutton (2005), self-harming behaviour does not have an explicit suicidal aim but represents a coping strategy used when dealing with psychological deprivation or when trying to regain a lost emotional balance. The invisible emotional pain thus transfers into a visible one in the form of physical injuries. In this context, Janis and Nock (2008) point to the fact that an individual planning a suicide is longing for death but a self-harming individual only wants to feel better. However, this presupposition does not exclude the fact that self-harming can precede a suicidal attempt and it relatively often does. Laye-Gindhu & Schonert-Reichl (2005) state in the results of their study that in self-harming individuals suicidal thoughts are present more frequently (83% as opposed to 29% of individuals who do not harm themselves). Similarly, they identified a majority of self-harming individuals in case of suicidal attempts (26% as opposed to 6% of individuals who do not harm themselves) and claimed that as high as 89% of adolescents who attempted suicide also harmed themselves. The occurrence of self-harm in personal anamnesis is also one of the most significant predictors of completed suicide, the risk of which grows up to ten times in self-harming individuals according to some authors (Hawton & Harris, 2007). According to Assarnow et al. (2011) self-harm in personal medical history is a more significant predictor of a suicidal attempt than a previous suicidal attempt[12].

Whether self-harm changes into a subsequent suicidal attempt, or not, greatly depends on a number of significant intervening influences. Nevertheless, its occurrence can be in this context considered a significant risk factor. The risk factors of self-harm and of a suicidal attempt can in some cases be the same; however, some of them are exclusive for the given behaviour. In their study, Hawton, Saunders and O'Connor (2012) identify risk factors of self-harm, which are common for suicidal behaviour as well. These factors are low socioeconomic status, parental problems (divorce, separation, death of one of the parents, mental illness of parents), family history of suicidal behaviour, interpersonal problems, psychological disorder of the individual, addictive drug abuse, or feeling of deep hopelessness. In contrast, self-harm was different from suicidal behaviour in predominance of gender (female gender is predominant in case of self-harm and male gender is predominant in case of suicide). In case of self-harm, the authors

12 The results of the study by Cooper et al. (2005) highlight the importance of early intervention after an episode of self-harm in a suicide prevention strategy.

state the following significant risk factors: other than heterosexual orientation, impulsivity, poor self-confidence, perfectionism, inability to solve problems, or experience of being bullied.

Lloyd et al. (2007) examined the differences between self-harming individuals who attempted to commit suicide and those who only harmed themselves. In the group with suicidal attempts, more frequent outpatient psychiatric treatment or hospitalisation and more frequent occurrence of suicidal thoughts were found in personal medical history. At the same time, individuals who carried out more serious types of self-harm and more differing ways of self-harm attempted to commit suicide more often. When examining the social context of self-harm, Glenn a Klonsky (2009) came to the conclusion that self-harming individuals who acted in this way on their own in privacy had a higher percentage of subsequent suicidal thoughts and suicidal attempts. Swahn et al. (2012) state that approximately 70% of repeatedly self-harming adolescents sometimes attempt to commit suicide. In their research study conducted on American adolescents, they found that 38.2% of those who had harmed themselves during the previous year attempted to commit suicide as well. Occurrence of both self-harm and suicidal attempts was more frequent in adolescents using alcohol and other drugs, in those who were abused during their childhood, and those who stated a higher level of depression and impulsivity and a lower level of self-efficacy and parental support. Hawton et al. (2012) state the existence of risk of potential suicidal behaviour especially in repeatedly self-harming adolescent boys (the risk is often higher in those who cut themselves than those who poison themselves). Also, the results of Tormoen et al. (2013) suggest that self-harming behaviour and suicidal attempts can have a common base. However, they also found that adolescents who, apart from harming themselves, attempt suicide show worse mental health, problematic lifestyle and more behavioural problems. Brausch & Gutierrez (2010) discovered other interesting difference between self-harming adolescents and those who attempted suicide. Those who only harmed themselves showed a lower level of depression and feelings of hopelessness and a higher level of parental support and self-respect than those who attempted suicide. These results suggest that with the increase of risk factors (e.g. depression, feelings of hopelessness, and other) and decrease of protection factors (e.g. parental support, self-respect, and other) an individual can go from healthy behaviour to self-harming and even to suicidal behaviour.

2 The Specifics of Self-Harm in Adolescence

The occurrence of self-harm is not strictly connected to adolescence – it occurs in childhood as well as in adulthood; however, in adolescence its occurrence grows significantly (Tick et al., 2008). The first episode of self-harm before the beginning of adolescence is usually very rare, but it can occur basically at any age (Lawrence et al., 2000)[13]. Currently, in non-clinical population of adolescents, this behaviour evidently occurs to a very similar degree as other forms of risk behaviour, which are closely related to this stage of development and, to a certain extent, are a part of it. Up to a point, these forms represent a natural part of development, in which an individual goes through the passage from childhood to adulthood[14]. A number of authors, who examine self-harm from a long-term perspective, perceive it as an extreme form of a rite of passage. For example, Conterio, Lader & Bloom (1998) in this context claim that the self-inflicted wounds can serve as a physical proof of the process of transformation, while other authors ascribe the development of risk behaviour in the given developmental stage rather to the inability to adequately regulate strong emotions (Walsh & Rosen, 1988) and the effort to adapt to stressful situations (Chowanec et al., 1991)[15].

Similarly to other risk and pathological forms of behaviour, self-harm is not only connected to a certain specific biological mechanism – it is a very complex phenomenon with multifactorial aetiology[16]. It is very difficult to determine which specific causes trigger the given behaviour and how exactly this form of behaviour serves the individual. The overview below summarises the basic characteristics of self-harm in adolescence in non-clinical population (see Table 2). These characteristics will be discussed in the following text.

---

13 In recent years, the start of the development of such behaviour has slowly been moving to a lower age limit (see chap. 3.2.).

14 Favazza (1998) came with an interesting view in this respect – he distinguishes between culturally given self-harming acts, for example initiation rites and indigenous rites of passage, which represent the passage from childhood to adulthood in specific cultures and which are basically missing in "modern society" and are not replaced by any adequate alternative, except for example a successful graduation from secondary school.

15 The specifics of adolescence will be discussed in chap. 3.7.

16 More details in chap. 3.2.

Table 2. Basic characteristics of self-harmers in adolescence

FACTOR	COMMENTS
AGE	Self-harm is more common in early and middle adolescence
SEX	Sex differences have not been consistently identified for self-harm, but a number of studies prove gender differences in the occurrence and ways of harming oneself
AETIOLOGY	The start of self-harm can be influenced by short-term as well as long-term factors, which can include significant biological, personal, social or family influences, or their combinations.
PSYCHIATRIC ILLNESS	Diagnoses associated with adolescent self-harm include major depression, anxiety, substance abuse, eating disorders and conduct disorder
PSYCHOSOCIAL AND SITUATIONAL RISKS	Recent loss or rejection, poor social support, family conflicts, poor communication with parents, availability of firearms, academic difficulties, gender identity conflicts, history of maltreatment, being bullied, risky behaviours, and exposure to self-harm in the community or media

2.1 Prevalence

For an extensive period, many research studies based their statements on prevalence of self-harm in adolescence on the conclusions of Favazza and Conterio (1988), whose estimation of prevalence was in the ratio of 750 cases per 100000 persons in the general population, as opposed to 1800 cases per 100000 persons in population of adolescents and younger adults (15–35 years of age). However, the authors based these numbers on the prevalence of disorders where, according to the DSM-III, self-harm appeared as a symptom[17] (Suyemoto, 1998; Messer & Fremouw, 2008). It is, therefore, not possible to use this finding as the basis for current research because many contemporary studies state a relatively high occurrence of self-harm even in non-clinical population of adolescents[18], which is the primary focus of this publication.

However, it is very difficult to determine the actual occurrence of self-harming behaviour in non-clinical adolescent population because the conclusions of

17 It was a borderline personality disorder, histrionic personality disorder, anti-social personality disorder, eating disorders, schizophrenia, serious episode of depression, and multiple personality disorder.

18 In psychiatric patients, the occurrence of self-harm in the period of adolescence is usually stated in the range of 40% (Darche, 1990) to 61% (DiClemente, Ponton & Hartley, 1991; Taiminen et al., 1998).

several research studies differ significantly. This fact is further negatively influenced by the inconsistent terminology related to this specific behaviour, heterogeneity of diagnostic or screening methods, which are used to identify self-harm (see Chap. 6), and the dissimilarity of broader socioeconomic and demographic conditions in which the current research studies are carried out.

The inconsistent terminology along with the use of dissimilar research method designs for identifying self-harm complicate comparing the results of various studies examining such behaviour. Muehlenkamp et al. (2012) carried out an analysis of studies concerned with the prevalence of this behaviour in the years 2005–2011, in which they point to the decreased prevalence of self-harm in research studies using one-item methods to determine the occurrence of this behaviour, compared to the results gained by methods comprising a complex list of individual forms of self-harm (e.g. in the form of listing) where the respondents marked their own experience with this behaviour. Also, Tormoen et al. (2013) comes to the conclusion that the use of simple questions in research can result in a false drop in the ascertained prevalence and thus in the underestimation of the seriousness of self-harm in adolescents.

Another problem is the very detection of this behaviour in non-clinical population by practicing specialists – especially doctors, psychiatrists and psychologists – because self-harming individuals who are not treated for any other diagnosis (e.g. depression, anxiety, or behaviour disorders) do not have to get in touch with them at all. Madge et al (2008) state that only one eighth (12.4%) of cases of self-harm leads to detection and subsequent hospitalisation. Other authors state an even lower number. The vast majority of self-harming adolescents thus never seek the help of psychologists, doctors or other adults (Hawton et al., 2012; Hrubá, Klimusová & Burešová, 2012), which also complicates the mapping of the real prevalence of this behaviour. Studies mapping prevalence of self-harm frequently focus on recent episodes (usually in the last 12 months), or on an individual's last experience with self-harm in general. With regard to the focus of this publication on non-clinical adolescent population, it discusses in the following pages only the results of research carried out especially in schools using the general population in this stage of development. Key studies, concentrating on clinical population and using data from outpatient intakes and hospitalisations, are included in Chapter 3.3.

González-Forteza et al. (2005), who studied self-harm on a sample of more than 2500 Mexican respondents at the average age of 15.7 years, state that lifetime prevalence of self-harm without suicide is 7.2%, whereas Portzky, De Wilde & van Heeringen (2007) state that the lifetime prevalence of self-harm in their group of adolescents is 10.4% in Belgium and 4.1% in the Netherlands (the research was carried out on the sample of 8889 respondents aged 12–18). However, the most frequently stated prevalence of this behaviour is between approximately 12% (Favazza & Conterio, 1989) and 35% (Gratz, 2001) – some authors move this range even between 14% and 41% (Paivio & McCulloch, 2004; Polk & Liss, 2007). Ross & Heath (2002) state at least one experience with self-harm in non-clinical adolescent population in 13.9% out of 440 examined persons. Muehlenkamp & Gutierrez (2004) claim a prevalence of 15.9% in American adolescents, while subsequent research in the USA done by Lloyd-Richardson et al. (2007) states up to 46.5% of adolescents with their own, at least one-time, experience with self-harm. Probably the highest occurrence of self-harm is presented by Dyl (2008), who claims that prevalence in the community of adolescents can reach up to 47%. A Norwegian research study (Kvernmo & Rosenvinge, 2009) found that in the researched population of adolescents, 12.5% of them stated that they harmed themselves. Plener et al. (2009) in the German study claim that 25.6% of adolescents have experience with self-harm. In the study by Hallab & Covic (2010), the authors learned that as high as 69% of respondents in non-clinical population of adolescents have at least one experience with self-harm. However, this high prevalence results from the fact that the authors of the study also included self-abasing thoughts (61%) and subsequent abuse of alcohol (58%). In the results of a research study conducted on a sample of over 17600 Chinese students aged 12–24 years, Wan et al. (2011) claim that the occurrence of self-harm during the last year before collecting the data was 17%. Swahn et al. (2012) put the prevalence of self-harming behaviour in more than 4100 respondents in the USA at 20.3%. In their survey, Hawton, Saunders & O'Connor (2012) claim that in a great majority of studies the occurrence of self-harm in adolescent population is around 10%. In an extensive Australian research (1943 adolescents), Moran et al. (2012) found self-harm in 8% of adolescents. In the more recent Norwegian research by Tormoen et al. (2013), the authors state the occurrence of self-harming behaviour only in 4.3% of adolescents (in a research group of 11440 respondents) and lifetime prevalence in 9.3%. Baetens et al. (2015) claim 13.41% lifetime prevalence in Belgian adolescents. Using a sample of 1131 Irish adolescents aged 11–13 years, Coughlan et al. (2014) in their recent study claimed that the occurrence of self-harming behaviour was 4.8% and 5.5% for suicidal thoughts.

An interesting insight on prevalence of self-harm was offered by a Japanese study from 2006 (Izutsu et al.), which lists the prevalence according to the different manners of self-harm (see Chap. 3.6). The prevalence of self-harm is also often studied in relation to gender differences in its occurrence. However, due to the above stated reasons, we find significant differences even in this area of its research in professional literature. While, for example, Gratz (2001) and other authors (Baetens et al., 2015) did not confirm differences in occurrence based on gender but only in differing frequency of occurrence of various manners of self-harm, Moran et al. (2012) in their study identified self-harm in 8% of respondents with a predominance of girls over boys (10% vs. 6%). Nevertheless, the most frequently stated ratio is 2–3:1 with a predominance of girls (Laye-Gindhu & Schonert-Reichl, 2005; Hargus et al., 2009; Madge et al., 2011; Burešová, Vrbová & Čerňák, 2015 and others – see Chap. 4. 1.). However, if authors of research studies also include indirect ways of self-harm (like smoking and excessive use of alcohol), the ratio reverses to 1–2 times higher occurrence of self-harm in boys (Izutsu et al., 2006).

The European study with the greatest scope so far, *Child and Adolescent Self-Harm in Europe (CASE)*, which was conducted in the years 2000–2001 on a sample of 30477 adolescents aged 14–17 years, finds 11.1% prevalence of self-harm (Hawton et al., 2002; Sullivan, et al., 2004; De Leo & Heller, 2004; Rossow et al., 2007; Madge et al., 2008; Scoliers et al., 2009 and others). The same research design was adapted in 7 countries, out of which 6 were European (Belgium, England, Ireland, the Netherlands, Hungary and Norway), and the seventh was Australia.[19] The study found that girls were twice as likely to exhibit self-harming behaviour than boys. The frequency of self-harming behaviour in girls and boys differed in different countries. The lowest observed occurrence of self-harm in girls in the last year was 3.6% in the Netherlands and the highest one was 11.8% in Australia. In the other four countries, the occurrence of self-harm in girls exceeded 10.4%. Its lowest observed occurrence in boys in the last year was 1.7% in Hungary and the Netherlands and the highest one was 4.3% in Belgium (Madge et al., 2008).

An analysis of studies on prevalence of self-harm in the years 2005–2011 was carried out by Muehlenkamp and her colleagues (2012). Their results, among others, highlight the decreased prevalence of self-harming behaviour in research studies which use one-item methods to determine the occurrence of this type

19 This study can be considered unique in the area of research on self-harm not only due to its scope and broad international cooperation but also due to the fact that prior to its beginning a pilot study was conducted where the respondents described the way they harmed themselves and based on their responses two independent evaluators, using 150 subjects, defined the criteria for what is regarded as self-harm. Subsequently, these criteria were used to sort and process the research results and the rest of the research file.

of behaviour, in comparison to the results gained from methods which included a complex list of individual manners of self-harm and the respondents marked their own experience. As this comparative study shows, in the last five years the prevalence of self-harm in adolescents has stabilised and it seems not to be growing. According to the authors of this meta-analysis, lifetime prevalence of self-harm was between 5.5% and 30.7% and its prevalence in the year before collecting the research data was between 7.3% and 37.2%. The data show that the occurrence of self-harm in non-clinical population of adolescents cannot be seen as marginal, and therefore it is absolutely necessary to pay due attention to this highly risky form of behaviour.

2.2 Aetiology

Middle and early adolescence is generally regarded as a crucial age for the development of self-harming behaviour (Kvernmo & Rosenvinge, 2009). Dyl (2008) presents the results of various studies in his work and observes that the usual prevalence of self-harm in adolescents is in a relatively broad range of 5–47%, 12–35% in university students and only 4% in adult population. Such distribution leads to the conclusion that the period of adolescence is very sensitive with regard to the development of self-harm and one of the crucial interests of specialists studying this area is to map the factors which influence its development because repetitive and long-term self-harm in adolescence often continues all the way to adulthood (Hawton, Saunders & O'Connor, 2012).

The results of the conducted research studies state that the first episode of this specific form of behaviour occurs at various ages. Some studies illustrate that the average age of the first act of self-harm could be in the period around 12 years of age (Lieberman, 2004; Izutsu et al., 2006; Kvernmo & Rosenvinge, 2009; Whitlock, 2010 and others), which also corresponds with the results of extensive Czech research (Burešová & Klimusová, 2014). Similarly to González-Forteza et al. (2005), Levenkron (1998) move this age limit to 13 years of age. Hawton et al. (2012) state the average age of development of self-harming behaviour between 12 and 14, Ross & Heath (2002) state the age of 14 as crucial and Kvernmo & Rosenvinge (2009) see the period between 13 and 16 years of age as the most crucial period for the development of this specific and risky form of behaviour. The results of Australian research by Moran et al. (2012), in this context, imply that later in the period of adolescence the frequency of occurrence of self-harm actually decreases. However, Hawton et al. (2013) claim that in their research conducted on a sample of 5205 subjects from non-clinical population, only 0.1% of self-harming children under the age of 10 were identified, 17.8% of self-harmers were at the age 10–14 years and 82.1% of them were 15–18 years old.

The factors influencing the development of self-harm are studied by a number of authors (Suyemoto & MacDonald, 1995; Dervic et al., 2004; Skegg, 2005; McMahon et al., 2010; Hsu et al., 2013 and others), who mostly agree in their works that the factors which affect the development of self-harm can be short-term as well as long-term and they can include biological, social, personal or family factors, or combinations thereof (for more details, see Chap. 3.7.). The biopsychosocial model of self-injury posits that the occurrence and maintenance of NSSI is the result of contributing factors from one of more of five domains: affective, behavioural, biological, cognitive and environmental. "These domains do not function in isolation and are intertwined and interact upon each other" (Heath & Nixon, 2009, p. 144).

Some of the *long-term factors* influencing development of self-harm are an early loss or separation from the primary carer, dismissive or overprotective upbringing approach, various forms of abuse and battering, permanent personality traits and mental illnesses. Some of the numerous *short-term influential factors* are, for example, problems in relationships with close persons, lack of social support, problems related to studies and health, abuse of drugs, and also worsening symptoms of a developing mental illness (Skegg, 2005). An important role in the development of this form of behaviour is played by *precipitating factors* – stress factors which occur several days before the first episode of self-harm. These include especially current problems in relationships with parents, peers, teachers, or a partner, bullying at school, death of a close person, a period of free time, weekends, holidays, serious financial problems, etc. It follows from the results by Portzky, de Wilde & van Heeringen (2007) that the risk of self-harming behaviour is raised by serious life events in the preceding year. The serious life events monitored in the research were problems and arguments with parents, friends and partners, suicidal attempts and a completed suicide in the immediate environment of the respondent and worries about sexual orientation. Most serious life events raised the risk of self-harming behaviour only if they did not happen earlier than the preceding year.

In the results of their research, Rissanen, Kylmä & Laukkanen (2008) divide the causes leading to self-harm into *external, internal* and *experience* factors. Some of the external factors were: exposure to violence, concrete life events, abuse of alcohol and other drugs, interest in Satanism, being informed about the possibility of self-harm, and arguments and conflicts with close persons. Some of the internal and experience factors leading to self-harm were the experience of conflicts, loneliness, changes in life, fear of violence, the experience of illness or being different from others, low self-esteem and negative emotions like fear, anger and bad mood.

The study by Janise & Nock (2008) focusing on the theoretical concept of self-harm also states several risk factors related to self-harm, such as: being of white race[20], being an adolescent, being of female sex and the experience of sexual abuse in childhood. In the European comparative study CASE, Madge et al. (2011) merged the serious life events contributing to the development of this risky form of behaviour into the following categories: problems with friends and peers; problems with or between parents; serious illness of a friend or within a family; physical or sexual abuse; suicide or self-harm of friends or within a family; death of a close person; worries about sexual orientation; problems with police; abuse; problems related to school. The most significant relation to self-harm was found in previous experience with self-harm or suicide and then in physical or sexual abuse, problems with friends and peers and problems with or between parents. The results of the previously mentioned European study CASE show that in the etiopathogenesis of self-harm an important role is played by personal traits as well as by stressful life events (Madge et al., 2011). Nevertheless, the trigger of self-harm, or one of the possible causes of the development of this behaviour, is also the actual start of adolescence related to turbulent hormonal and personality changes, transformation of relationships, etc. (Lieberman, 2004).

2.3 Comorbidity

For an extended period in the past, self-harm was connected exclusively with serious psychiatric diagnoses[21], developmental disorders[22], personality disorders, or suicidal tendencies (Zlotnick et al., 2003, Washburn et al., 2012). Psychologists and psychiatrists did not consider it necessary to distinguish self-harm as a separate diagnostic category and perceived it mostly as a phenomenon associated with, a number of areas of diagnoses. Even in the International Classification of Diseases (ICD) (2008), self-harm is seen as a non-specific or specific symptom of an otherwise diagnosable disorder. Therefore, self-harm was mostly perceived by professional as well as non-professional public as one of the symptoms of a number of mental illnesses, which mostly occur in borderline types of

20 The question is if other races are studied with the same intensity so that we can see the given statement as relevant.
21 See the previous text.
22 Mental retardation, autistic spectrum disorder, etc.

personality disorders involving emotional instability (Suyemoto, 1998; Evren & Evren, 2005; Messer & Fremouw, 2008 and others). At the same time, these authors state that a relatively high percentage of people who suffer from self-harming behaviour really belong to clinical population even though the causality factor in the interconnectedness of various types of mental disorders with self-harm remains unclear. In adolescent population of psychiatric patients, Rozsívalová, Trefilová & Paclt (2010) state up to 60% of prevalence of self-harm. Sutton (1999)[23] presents an overview of mental disorders diagnosed in deliberately self-harming individuals. Many other authors (see Tuisku et al., 2009) discovered a high correlation of self-harm and various other psychological problems, like depression, anxiety, bipolar disorder, and the already mentioned personality disorder. Due to the ongoing process of psychological development, personality disorders are not usually diagnosed until the age of eighteen – yet, self-harm in adolescence is often described in case of early diagnosis of personality disorders (Hawton, Saunders & O'Connor, 2012).[24]

However, the results of current research studies highlight the fact that self-harm does not have to be the equivalent to either one of the above-mentioned phenomena, even though it can accompany all of them. The behaviour, which until recently was considered by professional and non-professional public entirely highly pathological has, in the last years, become a norm in the population of adolescents to such an extent that 20% of adolescent individuals try it at least once in their life (Brunner et al., 2007; Jacobson & Gould, 2007; Swahn et al., 2012; Klimusová et al., 2014 and others).

Distinguishing self-harm as a separate diagnostic category, as suggested in the current DSM-V™ (2013), as well as differentiating between self-harming behaviour with and without the intention to die, as a part of the specification of its definition and terminology, brought a new perspective into these issues. It also resulted in the effort to classify it as an independent phenomenon – because apparently

23 From the group of neurotic disorders the following disorders appeared here: Post traumatic stress disorder, Panic disorder/generalised anxiety disorder, Obsessive-compulsive disorder, Multiple personality disorder, Depersonalisation and derealisation syndrome, dissociative disorder not further specified. From the group of emotive disorders we can find here the following: Depressive episode, Bipolar affective disorder and Dysthymia. The circle of personality and behaviour disorders includes Borderline-type emotionally unstable personality, Histrionic personality disorder and Non-specified personality disorder. Similarly, self-harm can occur in Schizoaffective disorder.

24 The issues of personality disorders, self-harm and childhood trauma are studied in detail in the work by Sansone & Sansone (2007).

it can often exist entirely independently and has its own specifics (Janis & Nock, 2008). Individuals who harm their own bodies but, at the same time, have no intention to take their lives have been repeatedly detected in both research and practice and have not been given any other clinical diagnoses (Hrubá, Burešová & Čerňák, 2015). Self-harming behaviour in these cases hardly ever threatens the life of the individual and in most cases does not even require hospitalisation. In this context, Skeeg (2005) states that self-harming individuals, even the chronic ones, are usually not psychotic and often have strong enough contact with reality to realise that their acts result in unsightly scars. The author also postulates an interesting thesis, stating that self-harm is not a disorder but a type of behaviour, which can be a symptom of clinical problems of various types or also a maladaptive response to various long-standing problems of an individual.

This assumption is also reflected in the occurrence of self-harm in adolescence, which in non-clinical population of adolescents can probably be identified either as an isolated phenomenon representing another form of risk behaviour (similarly to smoking, abuse of alcohol and addictive drugs, risky sexual activities, etc.), which is related to the development of adolescents and to a certain extent is basically usual in this developmental stage, or it can be related to other more significant clinical problems. In the study by Hrubá et al. (2015) conducted on a sample of 1110 adolescents aged 12–15 years both these forms of self-harm occurrence in adolescence were identified. The subjects who had never been treated by a psychologist or a psychiatrist claimed their own experience with self-harming behaviour in less than 20% of cases[25], while those who had been treated by such specialists claimed their own experience with self-harm in more than 40% of cases and were also more predominant in the group of adolescents who practiced this behaviour repeatedly, often and over an extensive period of time[26]. Ystgaard et al. (2009) claimed in this respect that only a small percentage of adolescents (12.2%) who harm themselves end up in a hospital or get appropriate care after such an act, which is also confirmed by the results of previously conducted studies (Hawton et al., 2002). According to the results of the research Burešová & Klimusová (2014), self-harming adolescents reveal these realities mostly to their peers, then parents and only a minority of them confide in doctors or specialists.

---

25 Which corresponds to the usual prevalence of this behaviour in this developmental stage.

26 This highlights the cyclical nature of self-harming behaviour described by Chapman, Gratz & Brown (2006) in his Experiential Avoidance Model (EAM) of deliberate self-harm.

Hawton et al. (2013) have done a comparative analysis of ten other research studies concentrating on the occurrence of previous self-harming behaviour in patients who were later diagnosed with a mental illness and entered hospital care. They found a coincidence of this behaviour with mental illness in 81.2% of cases in a group of adolescents in nine out of ten of the analysed research studies. Seven out of ten compared studies concerned mixed diagnoses of more disorders, most often mood disorders, especially depression, abuse of addictive drugs, anxiety disorders and attention disorders with hyperactivity[27].

Table 3. Prevalence of mental illnesses in self-harming children and adolescents (Hawton et al., 2013)

DIAGNOSIS	NUMBER OF STUDIES	OCCURRENCE %
Any mental disorder	9	81.2
Mood disorders	4	56.3
Depression	8	50.0
ADHD	3	24.0
Abuse of drugs	5	24.8
Anxiety disorders	4	16.6
Behaviour disorders	5	9.7
Adaptation disorders	4	24.7
Eating disorders	3	8.3
Bipolar disorders	2	7.3
Psychotic disorders	6	2.4

Comorbidity with Affective Disorders, Depressive Tendencies, Depression and Anxiety

Depressive tendencies and higher level of anxiety in self-harming individuals are described by many authors (Harrington, 2001; Ross & Heath, 2002; Sutton,

27 Jacobson et al. (2008) in a retrospective chart review study of 227 participants examined the psychiatric profiles of outpatient adolescents aged 12 to 19 years, engaging in different types of deliberate self-harm behaviours. Participants were divided into four groups: no deliberate self-harm, non-suicidal self-injury only, suicide attempt and suicide attempt plus NSSI. Those who attempted suicide were more likely to have major depressive disorder and/or posttraumatic stress disorder than those who engaged in NSSI only. Those who engaged in any type of DSH were more likely to have features of borderline personality disorder than those who did not engage in DSH. The suicidal ideation levels of those in the NSSI group were similar to those in the NoDSH group.

2005; Regner et al., 2012 and others). Self-harm in adolescence is very often connected with affective disorders, mostly with depressive symptoms, or even with an episode of depression[28]. Depression has been repeatedly found to be a risk factor influencing repetition of self-harm in adolescents (Hawton et al., 1999). Similarly to self-harm, this mood disorder is often relapsing and has tendencies to be chronic. However, according to Harrington (2001), self-harming individuals often have symptoms of depression, which in most of them do not fulfil the criteria for being diagnosed with a depression disorder. The connection between symptoms of depression at the age of 8 years and the occurrence of intentional self-harm at the age of 18 years is described by Tick et al. (2008) on the bases of a ten-year-long prospective study from the Netherlands. Brausch a Gutierrez (2010) in their study highlight the possibility of comorbidity of self-harming behaviour and depression and its symptoms – anhedonia, negative perception of the self, low self-esteem and higher amount of suicidal thoughts. According to Beatens et al. (2013), it is the higher level of self-criticism which supports the development of depression symptoms in self-harming individuals. Also the recently published Norwegian research study by Tormoen et al. (2013) states that there is a higher level of depressive tendencies in self-harmers in comparison to adolescents who do not harm themselves. Wan and his fellow researchers (2011) captured an interesting relationship between the frequency of self-harm and the occurrence of depression symptoms. In 90% of subjects, who did not harm themselves, the level of depressive tendencies was low whereas in self-harmers it was medium or high. Repeated self-harm was also connected to a high level of depressive tendencies.

In this context, some authors draw attention to significant gender differences in case of comorbidity of depression, anxiety and self-harm (Klonsky, Oltmanns & Turkheimer, 2003; Regner et al., 2012). Gunter et al. (2011) came to the conclusion that anxiety is even a better predictor of self-harm occurrence without the intention to die than depressive mood. Also Moran et al. (2012) in their extensive Australian research (1943 adolescents) learned that self-harm was connected with symptoms of depression and anxiety. Ross & Heath (2002) highlighted the significance of hostility in this context, when they identified only anxiety in 8.2% of self-harmers, only hostility in 26.2%, and found that as high as 54% of self-harmers manifested both hostility and anxiety in connection with the act of self-harm. However, most of the above stated authors agree on the fact that what is essentially important for the occurrence of self-harming behaviour is not the

28 In later age, comorbidity of self-harm and bipolar affective disorder is often found.

long-term state of an individual, but rather currently experienced stressful situations. Therefore, the reasons for comorbidity of depressive tendencies, depression and anxiety with self-harm have not yet been satisfyingly explained.

Comorbidity with Alexithymia

Alexithymia[29] is often connected with self-harm as one of the factors which contribute to its development (Zlotnick et al., 1996; Paivio & McCulloch, 2004; Hsu et al, 2013 and others) and, at the same time, it is relatively often found in individuals who used to be physically punished or abused in their childhood. Individuals who in their childhood experienced violence on their own body caused by other people (mostly people close to them) turn the anger against themselves in the period of adolescence and paradoxically continue the work of their tormentors. A number of research studies focusing on the motivation of such behaviour come to the same conclusion: such individuals adopted this type of behaviour towards their own bodies as normal and natural and neither their families nor the people closest to them let them know that such behaviour is not perceived and accepted as normal by the general public (Simpson & Porter, 1981; Suyemoto & MacDonald, 1995; Suyemoto, 1998 and others). Evren & Evren (2005) state that self-harming individuals have a problem to identify and describe their feelings. Based on a conducted research study, Hsu et al. (2013) claim that adolescents who harmed themselves also had a higher level of alexithymia, which was higher in boys. The authors of the study are also convinced that alexithymia does not have to be directly connected with self-harm, but it can play the role of a facilitator of self-harm in a disturbed relationship between a parent and a child.

Comorbidity with Posttraumatic Stress Disorder

Harned, Najavits &Weiss (2006) states that post-traumatic stress disorder (delayed and protracted reaction to a stressful situation which is exceptional or catastrophic), among other things, supports the development of self-harming behaviour. The typical symptoms, which occur as part of the attacks of self-harm provoked in this away, are nightmares, re-experience of the trauma, higher excitability, irritation and emotional numbness. Individuals with such a diagnosis who also harm themselves usually experienced a trauma in their childhood (serious

29 Alexithymia is an interesting phenomenon, which is classified as a borderline concept of psychosomatic medicine. Currently, it has been shown in several clinical disorders such as somatoform disorders, panic disorder, depression with dominance of vital and somatic symptoms, posttraumatic stress disorder and eating disorder (Vanheule, 2008).

neglect of care or physical or sexual abuse) and are also experiencing a trauma from their own self-harm at the moment (Miller, 1994). In this context, self-harm is understood as the ability to survive, with the aim to adapt and to disassociate oneself from unmanageable affective states. Sexual and physical abuse and bullying in childhood is associated with a broad scale of self-harming behaviour (Hawton et al., 2002; De Leo & Heller, 2004; Ystgaard et al., 2009 and others).

Comorbidity with OCD

Another typical illness where self-harm occurs relatively often is obsessive compulsive disorder, which is classified as an anxiety disorder[30]. It usually starts developing as early as in the period of pubescence and the most common forms of self-harm connected with OCD are: pulling out hair, eyelashes and eyebrows, compulsive piercing and removing and scratching of skin (Favazza, 1998). An obsessive-compulsive individual needs to gain control over the situation by using often even absurd rituals, through which he or she releases the tension. Therefore, it is possible that harming oneself is also a certain form of ritual, which makes the self–harming individual feel in control of the situation (Messer & Fremouw, 2008).[31] Yaryua-Tobias, Neziroglu & Kaplan (1995) came to an interesting conclusion in their research when they discovered that up to 70% of individuals suffering from OCD and harming themselves at the same time experienced sexual abuse in their childhood.

Comorbidity with Eating Disorders

This type of comorbidity is most often documented in connection with mental anorexia and bulimia (Yaryura-Tobias, Neziroglu & Kaplan, 1995; Matsunaga et al., 2000; Sansone & Levitt, 2002; and others). These authors highlight the phenomenological connection between the two phenomena[32] and also imply that there could even be a difference in the occurrence of self-harm between

30 Its symptoms are obtrusive thoughts (obsession) and subsequent compulsions, which is repeated, stereotypical, pointless and purposeless behaviour. Obsessions provoke anxie-ty in an individual, which he/she afterward lowers by subsequent compulsions. If an in-dividual attempts to face obsessions and subsequent compulsions, it makes him or her experience a relatively high level of anxiety.

31 However, if self-harm is a part of compulsive rituals, we cannot consider it comorbidity.

32 It is typical of both self-harm and eating disorders that they most frequently develop in early adolescence and they are both connected with the feelings of dissatisfaction with one's own body and personal incompetence.

purgative and non-purgative types[33]. Some authors state that more than a half of repeatedly self-harming girls also had or still have an eating disorder at the same time (Favazza a Conterio, 1989, Wonderlich et al., 2002; Claes & Muehlenkamp, 2014). Wiederman & Pryor (1996) identified comorbidity of self-harm with mental anorexia (14.6%) and mental bulimia (29.3%) in girls hospitalised in short-term hospital care for eating disorders (average age 15.44 years). Favazza (1996) identified as much as 73% of self-harmers with simultaneous eating disorders. Schulze et al. (1999) states in his context that up to 30% of adolescents, who suffer from eating disorders, showed marks on their skin caused by self-cutting, burning with a cigarette or hitting oneself. The occurrence of self-harm along with eating disorders is often connected with other risk factors in personal or family medical history (Paul et al., 2002; Cumella, Eberly & Wall, 2008; Hilt et al., 2008; Claes & Muehlenkamp, 2014).

Connection between Self-Harm and Addictive Disorder

Self-harm can also be closely related to addictive disorders. In this context, it is highlighted that the mechanisms accompanying self-harming behaviour are very close to the mechanisms accompanying addictions (Lieberman, 2004). Victor et al. (2012) focused on verifying the assumption that self-harm and addictions have a common basis and came to the conclusion that craving was significantly higher for addictive drugs and that the need to harm oneself was associated almost exclusively with the context of negative emotions, while the abuse of addictive drugs appeared in a broad variety of contexts. Nevertheless, in adolescents a connection is described between self-harming behaviour and abuse of alcohol and other addictive drugs, which are generally used more in this period (Glenn & Klonsky, 2012). Madge et al. (2008) learned that almost one fifth (19.9%) of episodes of self-harm happen under the influence of alcohol and one eighth (12.8%) under the influence of other drugs. Self-harm under the influence of addictive drugs is more frequent in boys – in case of alcohol it is 32.8% of boys as opposed to 15.6% of girls, in case of illegal drugs it is 26.2% of boys as opposed to 8.2% of girls. What has also been observed is a connection between the use of alcohol or drugs and a form of self-harm. A rather low control of impulsive behaviour is stated as a risk factor for this behaviour –a common coping strategy of

33 The restrictive type relies on a severe reduction in food intake, even starving, and excessive amount of exercise. The purgative type, also called bulimic, is characterised by alternating states of strict restriction in food and subsequent overeating, which they compensate by provoking vomiting.

putting up with emotional strain can be in the background (Hawton, Saunders & O'Connor, 2012).

Comorbidity of self-harm was monitored by many authors in different contexts as well and the conducted studies demonstrate a generally higher prevalence of self-harm in outpatients or individuals in hospital care. Lipschitz et al. (1999) identified it in 39% of adolescents accepted at a hospital crisis centre for adolescents, Healy et al. (2002) identified it in as high as 62.5% of adolescents checking into a mental health facility, Nixon, Cloutier & Aggarwal (2002) observed it in 29.7% of short-term hospitalised individuals at a psychiatric ward, and Cyr et al. (2005) in 62.1% of individuals accepted at a hospital crisis centre for adolescents.

2.4 The Progress of Self-Harm

The development and progress of self-harm are one of the few factors on which specialised literature agrees. If we use the framework of the current concept of self-harm described in the DSM-V™ (2013) diagnostic manual, we can build up on the fact that self-harming behaviour without the intention to die develops in the period of early adolescence, progresses in the period of middle adolescence and can continue for many years, lasting for weeks, months or years.

Already in the early 1990's, Tantam & Whittaker (1992) give two basic reasons why an isolated, often originally only experimental, experience with self-harm can grow into repeated self-harm, even becoming addictive. The first reason is a reduction of tension – self-harm is a socially acceptable response. The second reason is release – self-harm leads to an acceptable change of mood. This release can be caused directly by biochemical mechanisms, habitually or symbolically. Both these reasons can also be combined. According to Favazza (1998), episodic self-harm can become repeated, if it overtly fascinates a self-harming individual. The transition from episodic to repeated self-harm is mostly gradual and usually happens between the fifth and the tenth episode of self-harm. A self-harmer defines himself or herself as, for instance, a cutter or a burner. However, a clear causality between the mechanisms through which individual risk factors, described in Chapter 3.2., support the development, progress, and continuation of self-harming behaviour has, as of yet, not been documented. This is due to the fact that most of the conducted research has focused specifically on the mutual relationship between a concrete risk factor and self-harming behaviour, and detailed studies focusing on the mutual co-influence of various factors on the development of self-harm, also possibly resulting in the repetition of this behaviour, have been rare so far (Nock, 2012).

Based on functional analysis of self-harm and theory of learning, the Diagnostic and Statistical Manual of Mental Disorders, DSM-V™ (2013) claims that it is characteristic of the majority of self-harming behaviour to be cyclical. A self-harming individual usually does it for a concrete period of time, then stops and after some time starts doing it again. Repeated self-harm is connected with the feelings of urgency and craving and the final pattern of behaviour is, to a certain extent, similar to addiction when self-harming intensifies – e.g. the cuts are deeper and more frequent, and the positive and negative reinforcement, which is experienced during self-harm, can have influence on further deepening and continuation of self-harming behaviour. One episode of self-harm can therefore be one isolated act of self-harm as well as several such acts (Sutton, 1999). The frequency of such behaviour can differ highly interindividually – from several episodes a day to one or two episodes a month to several rare episodes in six months.

Sutton (2005) claims that the most common frequency of self-harming acts is two to three times a week. The frequency of self-harm significantly differs across individuals. Laye-Gindhu & Schonert-Reichl (2005), in this context, stated that in their research study they identified 52% of individuals who harmed themselves 2 to 10 times, 12% 11 to 20 times and 12% more than 20 times per week. On the whole, as high as 75% of self-harming individuals claimed they harmed themselves repeatedly. Madge et al. (2008) state that repeated self-harm occurs in more than a half of girls and boys from their research file. Plener et al. (2009) state that 9.5% of self-harming adolescents in Germany and the USA harm themselves repeatedly and more than four times a week. Ross & Heath (2009) learned that 13.1% of self-harmers practice this behaviour even more than once a day. In 27.9% of participants from their research file, the frequency of self-harm was several times a week, 19.6% harmed themselves several times a month, 18% claimed the self-harm was occasional and 19.6% stated they harmed themselves only sometimes. In an extensive Chinese research involving 17622 respondents, Wan et al. (2011) discovered repeated self-harm (twice and more) in approximately 75% of self-harmers (i.e. 12.8% of all respondents). Hawton et al. (2012) state that 53.3% of self-harmers harmed themselves repeatedly at least once in their lives and 17.7% harmed themselves repeatedly during the period of one year.[34] Baetens et al. (2015) discovered more than 6 episodes of self-harm in 43.75% of self-harming Belgian adolescents.

This perspective makes it clear how very risky this form of behaviour is. The frequency and intensity of self-harm can relatively easily grow to such a point that an adolescent loses control over the seriousness of his or her injury (Hawton, 2005), which can even have lethal consequences.

Significant interindividual differences can also be traced in the length of occurrence of self-harm during one's life. Favazza (1989) reports that this behaviour can occur for a very short time as well as for several decades; nevertheless, in most cases it naturally disappears after five to ten years. Sutton (1999), who studied the prognosis of the length of occurrence of self-harming episodes, in her research study identified 30% of individuals harming themselves for less than 5 years, 24% for five to ten years, and 19% for ten to twenty years – 27% of the participants were fighting this problem for more than twenty years. Some years later, this author came to the conclusion that recent studies reflecting the length of occurrence of this highly risky form of behaviour proved that it is relatively difficult to stop practicing this behaviour (Sutton, 2005).

Probably the best predictor of the risk of future self-harm is the presence of previous self-harm in one's medical history. Subjective expectations of a self-harming individual regarding the potential future self-harm hardly corresponds to the real prevalence of the phenomena in the future (Janis & Nock, 2008). This is why a number of authors strived for a description of a certain general profile of a chronic self-harmer (Miller, 1994; Levenkron, 1998; Nichols, 2000; Selekman, 2002; Levitt, Sansone & Cohn, 2004 and others), one of the key factors being, apart from a number of risk factors in family and personal medical history, the beginning of self-harm in early adolescence.

Self-harm is therefore probably used by non-clinical population of adolescents most often as a coping mechanism, or a temporary way of keeping control over one's own body, its limits and the surroundings. This behaviour often serves adolescents as a means to release tension, which is common at this stage of development full of stormy biological, cognitive, emotional and personality changes. Leibenluft, Gardner & Cowdry (1987) describes 6 stages which occur during the act of self-harm (see Figure 1).

---

34 The conclusions of research studies differ significantly based on the method which was used to identify the frequency of this behaviour – e.g. in an Irish research study, Coughlan et al. (2014) states that only 0.4% of adolescents from the researched group harmed themselves more than four times in the last year and 4.3% of them two to three times.

Figure 1. The stages of act of self-harm (Leibenluft, Gardner & Cowdry, 1987).

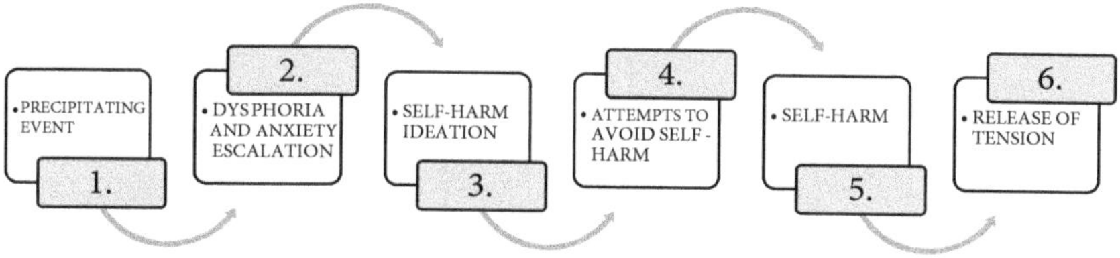

Claes & Vandereycken (2007) claim that the following psychological symptoms are present during the act of self-harm: 1. sudden and repeated obtrusive impulses to harm oneself, which the individual cannot resist; 2. feeling that an individual got into an unbearable situation which he or she cannot accept or control; 3. a higher level of anxiety, restlessness and anger; 4. limited cognitive-perception processes resulting in a narrowed view of the situation and possible alternative solutions; 5. feeling of mental relief after the act of self-harm and 6. depressive mood.

However, Sutton (2005) stresses that the act of self-harm has no limits and it is rather a cycle in which the particular behaviour is repeated for some time because even an odd episode of self-harm very often leads to another episode. Her model of the cycle of self-injury (see Figure 2) highlights the primary role of thinking in determining emotions and acts and describes the essential connections between individual phases of self-harm: *Mental anguish* (insistent and unacceptable thoughts, fantasies, memories and negative ideas of oneself create the feeling of an inner "chaos" which is accompanied by a strong emotional arousal), *Emotional engulfment* (strong unpleasant emotions and feelings, states of strong excitement and despair, an individual feels like exploding or suffers from the feelings of emptiness and unreality connected with dissociation), *Panic stations* (an individual has a strong feeling of losing control or strong feelings of derealisation and depersonalisation and experiences a strong urge to harm himself or herself in order to come back to reality and gain control), *Action stations* (the act of self-harm at the given moment diminishes the feeling of estrangement from reality, eases the inner pain – endorphins are released), *Feel better* (mental tension is released, an individual can feel joyful, relaxed, and can have the feeling of euphoria or numbness), *The grief reaction* (here comes the feeling of guilt because of the performed act, feelings of shame or disgust with oneself, an individual can experience the feelings of disappointment and negative thoughts appear again).

Figure 2. The cycle of self-injury (Sutton, 2005).

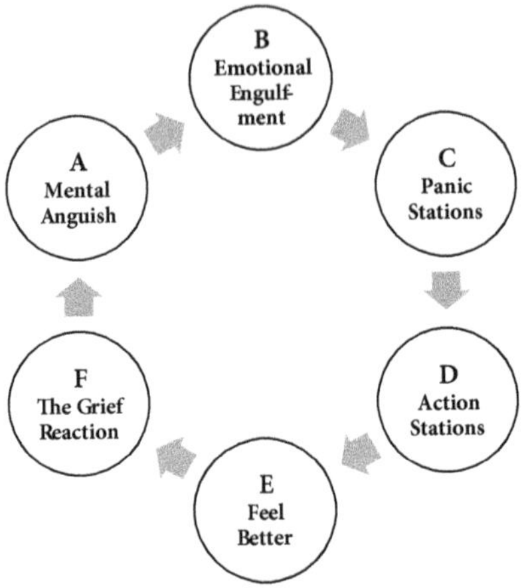

The individual act of self-harm is therefore only a short-time solution to a troublesome situation. Nevertheless, if the reasons which triggered it prevail, this risky behaviour in its consequence in some cases causes even bigger problems than those it originally aimed to solve. As the above-mentioned indicates, it would be wrong to assume that in the non-clinical population of adolescents self-harm is a rarely occurring and transient phenomenon. As such, it is often underestimated, especially by non-professional public, and it is perceived as merely a risky form of behaviour motivated primarily by the so-called adolescent defiance, or the effort to catch someone's attention – although this factor can also be a part of the motivation for the development of this form of behaviour in some adolescents as well as mere imitation of this behaviour when adolescents learn this problem-solving method from one another (De Leo & Heller, 2004)[35]. However, Hawton (2012) stresses that recurring episodes of self-harm are always alarming, especially in relation to a possible unintentional suicidal act since the frequency and intensity of this behaviour can escalate up to the point when an individual loses control over the seriousness of his or her injuries, which can have even fatal consequences. Fortunately, during the process of adolescence this behaviour probably gradually loses effectiveness as a coping mechanism in most adolescents and is gradually replaced by other, healthier, more adaptive and effective coping strategies, which is probably the reason why its occurrence gradually decreases in the following stages of development.

35 See the following chapter for more details.

2.5 Functions and Models of Motivation for Self-Harming Behaviour

One of the main questions, which scientists studying the phenomenon of self-harm repeatedly and tirelessly ask themselves, is one's motivation for this risky form of behaviour and its possible change. If we completely overlook mental illnesses, where self-harm occurs as one of their symptoms, then it is absolutely essential for understanding the causes of development of this behaviour to ponder upon the question of what makes otherwise healthy individuals violate the integrity of their own body and harm themselves and what function this behaviour actually has (Klonsky, 2007). In historical context, self-harm for a rather long time was related first to the *psychoanalytic sexual model* and it was understood as a possible solution to the Oedipal complex[36]. Subsequently, the view of self-harm and its function to a certain extent copied the gradual changes in approaching psychological phenomena in the context of the prevailing trends in psychology and their theoretical bases.

Individuals who harm themselves very often see themselves as isolated and detached from others (Himbert, 1994) and often give a great variety of motives leading to this risky form of behaviour – from the need to punish oneself to reduction of tension, aggression and emotional numbness, to improving one's mood, diminishing the feeling of loneliness, depersonalisation[37], or taking one's mind off unmanaged emotions, or the effort to force others to provide social support (Herpetz, 1995). Vanderlinden & Vandereycken (1997) sum up the reasons for self-harm into a functional scale according to direct impact on one's mental state. The scale is ordered from positive impacts to destructive ones: Relaxation (brings pleasure from pain and blood, reduces tension by direct abreaction through releasing endorphins after an algic stimulus) → Gaining attention (getting self-confirmation or protection) → Stimulation (feeling one's body or identity with the aim of escaping from dissociation → Punishment (due to guilt, feeling of weakness or lack of discipline) → Self-destruction (with the aim to lose attractiveness or parasuicide). A number of writers then perceive the function of self-harm primarily as a means to express

36 Friedman et al. (1972) state in their work that adolescents who are aware of an increase of sexual fantasies about their mother and at the same time have aggressive impulses, can perceive this as overwhelming. They can feel their bodies even "urge" them to have these fantasies and self-harm is an attempt to purge or destruct oneself, or at least purify one's body, which is perceived as separated from the self.

37 In this case, blood from the wounds works as a shock mechanism, which brings an indi-vidual back to reality and into his or her own body. Scars assure continuity of one's ex-istence since they link individual episodes of self-harm (Messer& Fremouw, 2008).

emotional pain and stress and to regulate affect (Solomon & Farrand 1996; Gross, 1999; Kench & Irwin, 2000; Klonsky, 2009 and others).

Systematisation of models explaining the function of self-harming behaviour (see Figure 3) was offered by Suymoto (1998) in her survey study. She suggested 4 basic functional models of self-harm (Environmental model, Drive model, Affect regulation model and Boundaries model) and subsequently classified theoretical approaches to this behaviour into 6 basic models, which were later used as a basis by many other writers.

Models of environment are focused on the interaction of a self-harming individual with his or her environment. They combine theories based on behavioural and systemic tradition, which presuppose the influence of social learning on the development of self-harm. Theories of social learning and operant conditioning explain how particular behaviour starts, what factors maintain it and what function this behaviour has in a broader system of an individual (family, peers, school etc.)[38].

Anti-suicidal model is based on psychoanalytic theory and it is perceived as a compromise between life instinct and death instinct and as an effort to avoid complete self-destruction – this behaviour gives the individual the feeling of control. In this conception, it is therefore an active, self-destructive coping mechanism averting the threat of real suicide. *This model is classified as the Drive model.*

Sexual model is also based on psychoanalytic theory and recognises various causes of the development of self-harm. It can be sexual satisfaction, control over sexuality and its development, the effort to avoid sexual activities, or even the thought of them.[39] This model is also classified as the Drive model.

Affect regulation model considers self-harm as means to regulate emotions, or express an inner conflict, or a conflict with one's environment. This model presupposes that individuals with tendencies to self-harm need a physical proof of emotional pain so that they themselves as well as others can perceive it as real.[40]

---

38 The reason why this behaviour develops and stays is the fact that it often diverts one's attention from real, and often more serious problems, and thus maintains homeostasis of the system.

39 An interesting connection related to self-harm was found in girls in the context of negative reaction to menarche (Rosenthal et al., 1972; Simpson, 1975; Doctors, 1981). Self-harm was perceived as a means to transform the passive into the active and therefore to transfer menstrual bleeding to a different place which is visible and can be controlled.

40 Some research studies (Leibenluft, Gardner & Cowdry, 1987) speak about self-harm as of a way of expressing emotional pain for the environment in a visual and comprehensi-ble manner. Clearly visible damage of one's body can be, for a self-harmer,

Dissociative model is based on dissociation very frequently described by self-harming individuals, and it assumes that this behaviour serves to maintain one's own self – one's consciousness. This model is focused on the relationship to oneself and on the inner experience and recognition of one's own self. Regarding this model, there is a lack of consensus among various authors about the function of self-harm – for some, self-harm ends dissociation (Pao, 1969; Simpson & Porter, 1981) and for others, on the contrary, self-harm starts it (Himber, 1994). It is often classified as the Affect regulation model.

Borderline model also concentrates on the need to confirm the limits of the self, but it is primarily focused on the relationship between an individual and his or her environment and on the unclearly set boundaries of the self. Here self-harm serves to define one's own borders – skin is perceived as the basic borderline between the self and others, and blood or scars are an indicator of a real existence of one's self. This model is also sometimes called Interpersonal boundaries model, or Boundaries model.

Figure 3. Functional models of deliberate self-harm (Suymoto, 1998).

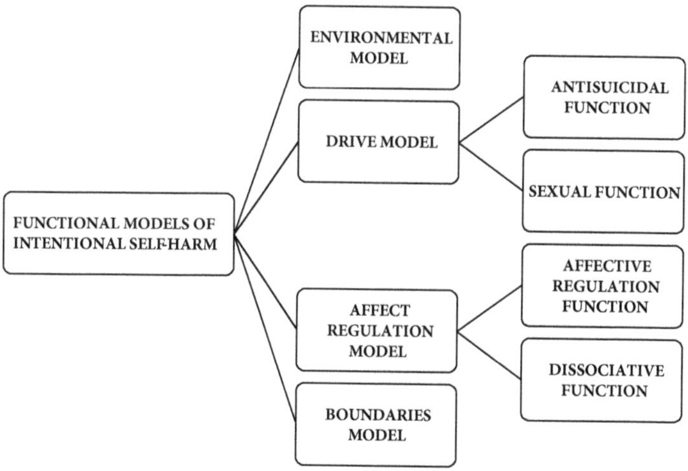

According to Brown (2002), it is possible to see the *Reinforcement model* as crucial in the context of self-harm – an individual can perform this behaviour in order to

---

a symbolical representation of his or her pain and at the same time a real physical proof of an emotional injury.

get a secondary positive reward (e.g. in the form of attention of his or her family, friends or caring personnel), or to eliminate some negative factors (e.g. reduce one's responsibility). The Reinforcement model, based on empirically verified results, was presented by Nock & Prinstein (2004). Their biaxal model is based upon two major areas of behaviour which maintain self-harm – social (interpersonal) and automatic (inner) behaviour – and on positive and negative reinforcement of this behaviour. By combining these two, 4 categories of behaviour are created: Automatic-negative reinforcement (this function of self-harm is most commonly presented in theoretical literature – an individual who harms himself or herself does it in order to get rid of tension, or other unpleasant feelings, therefore the aim is to regulate unpleasant feelings), Automatic-positive reinforcement (in this case self-harm serves as a means to trigger emotion, therefore the aim is to stimulate pleasant feelings), Social-negative reinforcement (the function of self-harm in this case is the effort to avoid a particular activity) and Social-positive reinforcement (the function of self-harm is to get attention from others).

Figure 4. Model of self-harm (Nock & Prinstein, 2004).

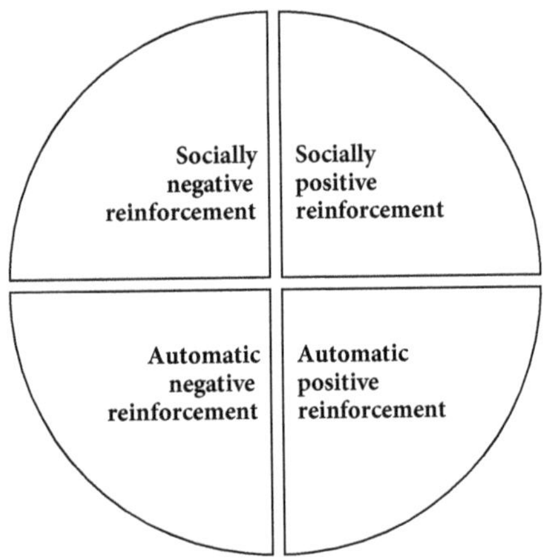

Empirical research of the authors of the model confirmed the validity of all the categories they present. Also, mapping of external motives leading to self-harm and the analysis of frequency of the stated items for individual categories are a valid contribution[41]. This model was subsequently verified by other authors,

41 The items related to automatic reinforcement were stated more often than the items re-lated to social reinforcement, and the results of the research showed that individuals

e.g. Lloyd-Richardson et al. (2007), who divided the group of self-harming adolescents into those who harm themselves gently, in a medium way, and seriously. Adolescents who harm themselves in a gentle way only stated automatic negative motives, while those who harmed themselves in medium and serious ways stated the influence of all of the above-mentioned motivation factors. The authors of the study also observed interesting differences in motivation of self-harming behaviour in relation to gender. In boys, social reasons were more frequent ("to make somebody in their surroundings angry"), while in girls the reasons were more often intrapersonal ("to punish myself"). Tan and his colleagues (2012) also identified a predominance of interior reasons, therefore, focus on regulating emotions, which can mean that the main aim of the majority of adolescents is the need of emotional and physiological regulation, meaning regulation and also reinforcement. In 73.3% of self-harmers, the authors found negative automatic reasons (reduction of negative feelings) and in 86.7% also automatic positive feelings (stimulation of pleasant feelings). Less than 50% of self-harmers stated social reasons (negative or positive). Similar results were also found by research authors Hrubá, Burešová & Čerňák (2015), which identified differences between individuals who harmed themselves one time, or repeatedly. Inner motives prevailed significantly in the group of researched individuals with the highest frequency of self-harm using more serious ways of self-injury (e.g. cutting), while in the group with experimental experience with such behaviour social motives were often found as well. Although these influences can be the factors which support such behaviour, they are probably not the primary cause of development of self-harm (Nock & Prinstein, 2004; Laye-Ginhu & Schonert-Reichl, 2005). This claim is also supported by the conclusions of Lieberman (2004) and Sutton (2005), who clearly show that only in a very small percentage of self-harmers the reason for self-harm is the need to get attention. It also corresponds with the fact that the majority of self-harmers make an effort to hide the effects of self-harm, which is, among others, also reflected in the choice of the area where they harm themselves.[42]

It is important to mention that *self-harm* can be perceived also as *a certain way of communicating with the surroundings*, or a means through which the social surroundings of an individual gets information about the emotions of the

---

who harm themselves state more internal reasons, which serve to regulate affects in their behaviour, than external reasons, by which they would influence the behaviour of others.

42 Self-harmers practice this behaviour in secret, alone, or e.g. in school restrooms, empty locked rooms and remote places. They also carry out self-harm primarily on those parts of their bodies which they can easily hide.

self-harmer[43]. Doctors (1981), in this context, states that these individuals usually have problems with expressing the emotions they experience and Richardson (2004) highlights that this fact is often wrongly confused, by professionals in clinical practice, with the effort to manipulate one's surroundings, which can even result in an insensitive approach to such an individual.

In the context of the development of self-harm, a number of authors see the Contagion model as a valid one as well. This model presupposes that an individual begins self-harming after he/she has been exposed to an act of self-harm, in other words, that he/she has seen another person harm himself or herself. This model was also considered by Walsh & Rosen (1985), whose work was followed by many other authors. Despite the relatively high number of studies describing the functioning of the Contagion model specifically in adolescence (Conterio, Lader & Bloom, 1998; De Leo & Heller, 2004), when adolescents "learn" this type of problem-solving mechanism from one another and from the media[44], this model is, however, also questioned by many other authors. This is due to the fact that the above-mentioned studies often disregard a great number of other significant variables and that this assumption has not been confirmed by other studies (Favazza et al., 1989; Nixon, Cloutier & Jansson, 2008) because the great majority of participants claimed that the thought of self-harm simply came to them and they were not influenced by any other people, media or literature. Apparently, it is possible to assume that the behaviour of these individuals can still be influenced by their surroundings without them taking notice, or that the impact of their surroundings is something to which they do not want to admit (Power & Brown, 2010).

The *Learned behaviour model* is important for the development of self-harm with traumatic aetiology. It is based on reinforcing this behaviour not only through the self but also through the closest surroundings of an individual and behaviour modelling. The model builds upon the assumption that self-harm starts through the experience of self-harm injury and leads to the persuasion that to feel injury is right or that one deserves it, or to the state when he/she finds the result of self-harm desirable (Himber, 1994; Suyemoto, 1998; Power & Brown, 2010 and others). Nevertheless, with regard to multifactorial aetiology of self-harm, this model again covers only some of the possible functions of this behaviour, and it can also include *observational*

---

43 The adolescent demonstrates his or her problems in this manner and therefore it is a certain "call for help in a hopeless situation" (Favazza, 1998).

44 Copy-cat effect (De Leo & Heller, 2004) is then spread especially through popular music, which is to a great extent infiltrated by self-harm, and it is made responsible for a higher prevalence of self-harm in adolescence.

learning in deliberate self-harm, where vicarious reinforcement is applied by observing the causal relationship between self-harm and its result in another person (Hawton, 2005).

On the other hand, Sutton (2005) sees self-harm as a very complex phenomenon and suggests the integrating model – The eight C's of self-injury. This model includes eight basic functions of this behaviour as they are often individually described by other writers in their theoretical bases: Coping and crisis intervention; Calming and comforting; Control; Cleansing; Confirmation of existence; Creating comfortable numbness; Chastisement and Communication.

Chapman, Gratz & Brown (2006) describe *The Model explaining triggering and maintaining of self-harming behaviour as avoiding unpleasant feelings* (Figure 5). This model integrates the above-mentioned Sutton's view on the function of this behaviour as well as the elements of the Reinforcement model by Nock & Prinstein (2004), and also synthesises the crucial parts of some other models in a complex way. According to the authors of the EAM model, self-harm, therefore, functions as an effective means to regulate negative emotions, thoughts, or a social situation. The model, at the same, time explains the principle through which self-harm is automated and becomes a routine solution to emotionally charged situations, in other words, a coping strategy or a learned behaviour.

Figure 5. The experiential avoidance model of deliberate self-harm (Chapman, Gratz & Brown, 2006).

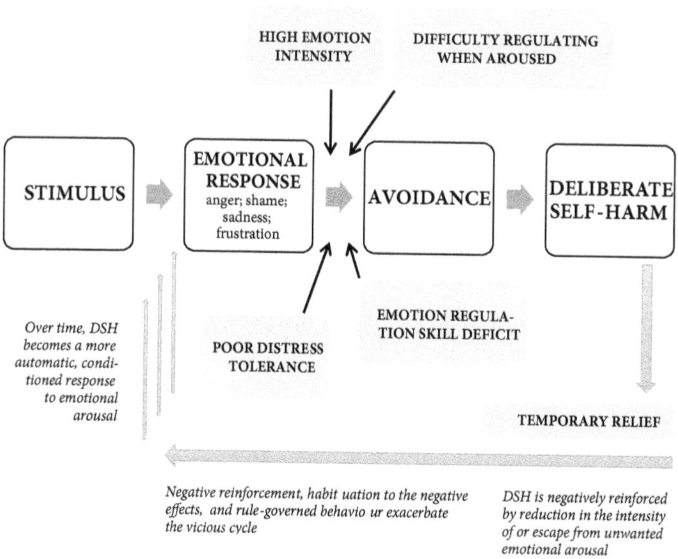

Bywaters and Rolfe (2002) created a list of motivations and functions of deliberate self-harm, where they described a relatively broad range of what can make a person engage in self-harm. Their unsorted categories include feelings of self-hate, self-punishment, venting of anger and resentment, coping strategy, but also for instance serious stress, rape or bullying, and they state that the development of this behaviour can have motives like taking control, perceived disinterest of one's surroundings, the intention to shock the surroundings, etc.

Power and Braun (2010) present a very clear division of models explaining the function of self-harm while building upon the primary functions of this behaviour (Figure 6).

Figure 6. Functional models of self-harm according to Power & Brown (2010).

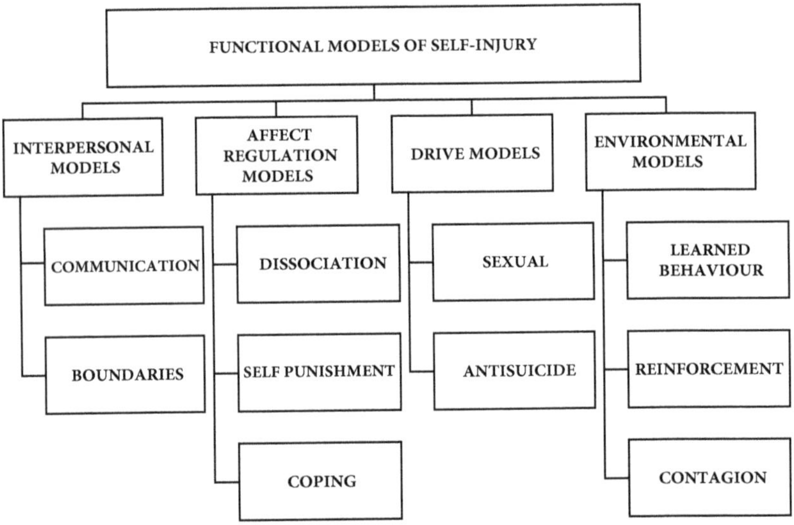

One can find a number of studies focusing on the functions of self-harm (Himber, 1994; Herpetz, 1995; Gross, 1999; Lieberman, 2004; Madge et al., 2008; Klonsky, 2009; Whitlock, 2010 and others) and it is apparent that all the above-mentioned motives to a certain extent run through all the mentioned functions of this behaviour, which is based on multifactorial aetiology of self-harm. This conclusion is also supported by the results of current research studies carried out in this area. Madge and her colleagues (2008), who were comparing the reasons leading to self-harm as a part of the above-mentioned European study CASE on a sample of 30477 adolescents. Based on their analysis, they classified some of the most commonly stated reasons as: the desire to free oneself from negative feelings, to punish oneself, or to die. The less frequent reasons were the need to scare someone, to seek attention or to gain something back. Most respondents stated more than one reason to self-harm at once, which is based on a multifactorial cause of this type of behaviour, in which there is more often a combination of several motives for self-harm rather than one isolated reason. The authors further highlighted the fact that reasons to self-harm are connected with the chosen manner of self-harm – e.g. cutting was closely related to the need to punish oneself in a group of girls.

Whitlock (2010) claimed that the most frequent reason for self-harm is experience of a strong negative emotion, or exposure to emotional pressure, and other problems in the area of emotions; emotional flattening and anhedonism also play a role here. Self-harm can therefore be used as a means of dealing with anxiety, releasing negative feelings or relaxing in a stressful situation (Kvernmo & Rosenvinge, 2009), but its aim can also be gaining control over one's own body and mind as well as the desire to punish oneself. Sometimes a deliberate re-experience of trauma occurs as a part of the act of self-harm, so that the individual can gain control over himself or herself. In this context, Pearlman (1997) has already claimed that in some individuals self-harming behaviour can develop partly due to the fact that they have not found a different way of dealing with problems and strong emotional stress in their life – this risky form of behaviour can therefore be triggered by many different stress factors (see Chap. 3.2. above). Beatens et al. (2013) observed Belgian adolescents and learned that up to almost 45% of them deal with unpleasant feelings through self-harm, almost 47% use this behaviour to gain control over their emotions, or to deal with anger (34.7%) and frustrations (32.7%), and to reduce stress and tension (32.7%).

The already mentioned DSM-V™ (2013, p. 803) approaches motivation to self-harming behaviour on the basis of 2 fundamental theoretical models of self-harm, which are based on functional behavioural analysis – the Reinforcement model and the theory which considers self-harming behaviour a form of self-punishment, in which the punishing action is supposed to balance the acts which have caused the distress or hurt other people.

Across the above-mentioned theoretical approaches to self-harm represented by their functional models, such realities as frequency of its occurrence or manners of self-harm seem significant when identifying the function of the given behaviour. Nevertheless, multifactorial aetiology of this behaviour does not allow for any clear causal conclusions about individual causes because the motives for self-harm very often cumulate and can change during the period when an individual harms himself or herself. Also, the functions which the act of self-harm fulfils for an individual, the frequency of self-harm, or the forms of self-harm can, to a certain extent, vary in an individual according to the current situation.

2.6 Forms of Self-Harm

Individual forms of self-harm can be systematized from several perspectives. In professional literature, this behaviour is most often divided into two basic types: self-poisoning (or overdosing) and self-mutilation (Sutton, 2005; Duffy, 2006). In non-clinical adolescent population, the occurrence of self-injury is identified more frequently than self-poisoning (overdosing). Hawton et al. (2002) states that the difference in occurrence of these two forms is at the ratio of 2:1[45]. Furthermore, self-harm can be classified according to the seriousness of injury – as we can see in Favazza (1998) and subsequent studies.

Table 4. Division of forms of self-harm according to the seriousness of injury (Favazza, 1998)

FORM OF SELF-HARM	OCCURRENCE	SERIOUSNESS OF INJURY
Major self-mutilation	It occurs the least often and appears during psychotic states or acute intoxication	A large part of tissue is damaged, usually even an amputation or castration is needed, and it results in permanent serious health injury.
Stereotypical auto-mutilation	It most often occurs in individuals with mental diseases, e.g. autism, mental retardation, etc.	Fixed patterns of behaviour occur here – banging one's head, biting one's fingers etc.
Superficial (mild) auto-mutilation – compulsive (close to OCD), impulsive[a], episodic (immediate response to an impulse)[b], repetitive (repeated impulsive reaction to stress factors)	It most often occurs in individuals in whom no serious mental disorder had been diagnosed – as an isolated episode or a type of behaviour repeated for a certain period of time.	The injury does not have fatal consequences – they are most often superficial injuries in the form of cuts, bloody scratches and blows to the head, etc.

Note. [a] Sutton (2005) describes this behaviour as rather spontaneous without significant prior planning and thinking about the consequences of the self-harming act. [b] Episodic self-harm happens without prior planning, brings quick and short-term relief from unpleasant emotions. The most common episodic self-harm is cutting or burning (Favazza, 1998).

45 However, clinical studies show many more cases of self-poisoning. Individuals who use an overdose of drugs need doctor's assistance much more often than individuals who cut themselves superficially or lightly burn themselves (Taiminen et al., 1998).

Lloyd-Richardson et al. (2007) also divide self-harm according to its form into minor (minor NSSI) and moderate to severe (moderate/severe NSSI). They classify hitting oneself, pulling one's hair, biting oneself, inserting objects under one's nails and skin and irritating wounds and the skin in order to promote blood circulation in the tissue as minor forms. They include cutting, burning, self-tattooing, scratching and erasing (i.e. rubbing an eraser over one's skin in order to cause burns and bleeding), among the more serious types of self-harm. The minor form of self-harm was observed by the authors of this study in 40.5% of self-harmers (18.8% of the whole group of 633 adolescents) and the more serious forms in 59.5% (27.7% of all researched adolescents). Adolescents practicing more serious forms of self-harm harmed themselves significantly more often and used various forms of self-harm, as opposed to the group using minor forms[46].

Other authors use different approaches to dividing individual forms of self-harm – according to various aspects. Koutek and Kocourková (2003) distinguish five basic areas of self-harm (Table 5).

Table 5. Forms of self-harm according to Koutek & Kocourková (2003)

FORMS	TERMINOLOGY	DESCRIPTION OF SELF-HARM
Auto-mutilation	Self-Mutilation	It most frequently occurs in patients with schizophrenia-type disorder, in personality disorders in general, especially in serious stressful situations and with sexual sadomasochistic practices. It is mostly based on psychotic disorder and can have symbolic meaning[a].
Self-harm	Self-Harm Self-Injury Self-Wounding	It occurs in personality disorder, mostly of borderline character. It is conscious, deliberate, frequently repeated self-harm without conscious suicidal motivation, when the integrity of one's body is damaged without a serious lethal impact[b].
Syndrome of deliberate self-harm	Deliberate Self-Harm	It occurs in personality disorders, eating disorders and in addictions to drugs. It represents a broader concept of self-harming behaviour separated from the category of suicidal attempts.

46 Diagnostic and Statistical Manual of Mental Disorders (2013) also links the use of various different forms of self-harm with a higher risk of psychopathology and potential suicide.

FORMS	TERMINOLOGY	DESCRIPTION OF SELF-HARM
Wrist cut syndrome	Wrist-Cutting Slashing	Cutting, especially wrist and forearm cutting, without a conscious suicidal tendency, dominates here. This behaviour is often of cyclical character.
Drug overdose	Self-Poisoning Overdosing	Non-indicated overdose of drugs without a clear suicidal intent. This behaviour is often repeated.

Note. [a] It is demonstrated through e.g. damaging a part of one's body, like genitals or hands. It is caused by pathological feelings of guilt and self-punishing, e.g. also during serious depression.
[b] The most frequent injuries are damaged skin, burns and drug overdose. The usual motive is the feeling of being angry with oneself, or relief from tension.

The preference to use particular forms of self-harm is very often examined, especially as a part of prevalence of this risky behaviour, and it is possible to observe significant, especially gender, differences here (see below). In non-clinical population, the most frequently stated forms of self-harm are related especially to the use of sharp instruments – cutting, or scratching until bleeding[47]. Some other very frequent forms of self-harm are self-hitting without a specific location, biting oneself and abuse of drugs (Ross & Heath, 2002; Sutton, 2005; González-Forteza et al., 2005; Wan et al. 2011 and others). Ross & Heath (2002) state that the most frequent form of self-harm is self-cutting – in 41% of self-harmers.

The traditional forms of self-harm according to Lieberman (2004) include especially cutting, burning, hitting, poking, hair pulling and head banging. In the research by De Leo & Heller (2004), cutting wounds, drug overdose, drug abuse, deteriorating state of health, hanging oneself and sniffing and inhalation appeared among the main methods of self-harm. Also in the research by Laye-Gindhu & Schonert-Reichl (2005), self-cutting was the most frequent form of self-harm (it included scratching and poking as well) – in 43%, then hitting oneself (26%), drug abuse (16%), problems with eating (7%), risky behaviour (5%) and breaking bones, falls and jumps stated by 3% of the respondents. It was

47 Individuals who harm themselves and use self-cutting during the act often state their behaviour has a symbolical meaning and claim that they feel better thanks to this type of self-harm because they gain the feeling of self-control in this way. This form of self-harm provides them also with the feeling of safety and exceptionality and reduces their feeling of inner emptiness thanks to pain and blood. Some of these individuals state they need to cut themselves because they have been invisible for too long and this behaviour brings them the mentioned feeling of exceptionality (Favazza, 1998).

followed by self-hitting in 32.8%, pinching in 6.5%, scratching in 5% and biting in 5% of self-harmers. Some other techniques used during self-harm include skin piercing, self-burning, self-scalding, disrupting the process of healing of previous injuries, or tampering with healing wounds, pulling or pulling out one's hair, eyelashes and eyebrows, consumption of a toxic material, or eating a non-edible object. Breaking bones, swallowing objects, inserting sharp objects under the skin or into body orifices occur rarely[48]. Madge and her colleagues (2008) in their research study claim that the stated motives for self-harming behaviour correspond with the chosen form of self-harm[49]. Whitlock (2010) in her study concentrating on self-harm highlights that she managed to document more than 16 forms of self-harm, adding creating bruises by hitting with various objects to the previous list of the most common techniques of self-harm. Also, it very often happens that a self-harming individual combines various forms of self-harm (Hawton et al., 2002).

The occurrence of individual forms of self-harm in adolescence: Laukkanen and her colleagues (2009) describe the occurrence of self-cutting in 11.5% of respondents, while other forms of self-harm reached the level of 10.2% (the research included over 6400 respondents from Finland in the age range of 13–18 years and observed a lifetime prevalence according to the type of self-harm). In an extensive Czech research, Burešová & Hrubá (2012) describe the three most common techniques of self-harm: scratching until bleeding (53%), hitting oneself (48%) and wrist cutting (45%). Hallab & Covic (2010) identified relatively high levels of occurrence of head banging, which they observed during the last year in 47% of respondents, self-hitting in 46%, scratching in 38% and self-cutting in 34% of subjects. The most addictive and most frequent form of self-harm, which occurred more than five times in one subject, was scratching in 60% of respondents, and self-cutting in 52%. The research study by Hawton and his team (2010) confirms that the two most frequent forms of self-harm in adolescents are self-cutting and overdose. As the work of Hrubá (2011) illustrates, scratching until bleeding (53%) predominates in Czech adolescents, followed by

---

48 The most frequently used tools are razors for self-cutting and a lighter or matches for self-burning. Individuals mostly harm themselves on the upper extremities, especially in the area from the wrist to the elbow. Self-harm in the area of lower extremities is also relatively common, especially on thighs. Only then follow the chest, mostly breasts in women, the area of stomach, palms, head, and the least frequent is self-harm in the area of genitals (Sutton, 1999).

49 For example, self-cutting is significantly related to the need to punish oneself in the population of girls.

deliberate self-hitting (48,5%) and wrist-cutting (45,5%). Also, the Australian research study by Moran et al. (2012)[50] describes self-cutting and burning oneself as the most frequent form of self-harm in adolescence. A Singaporean research study by Tan et al. (2012) described self-hitting as the most frequent form of self-harm (in 70%), followed by self-cutting (in 66.7%) and biting (in 56.7%). The Belgian research study by Baetens et al. (2015) claimed that the most frequent form of self-harm in adolescents is scratching until bleeding (50%). Despite the fact that self-cutting is usually the most frequent form of self-harm, as the above-mentioned results show, the most frequent form of self-harm which requires medical service is self-poisoning. Harrington (2001) states that approximately 90% of cases of self-harm accepted into hospital were cases of self-poisoning. Saçarçelik et al. (2011) supports this conclusion by claiming that the most frequent form of self-harm is drug abuse in self-harming hospitalised girls (73.3%) and self-cutting in boys (66.7%).

The occurrence of individual forms of self-harm according to gender: in general, men tend to use various forms of self-torture (e.g. self-hitting), while women more frequently cut themselves. These are followed by skin piercing and scratching in both sexes alike (Bywaters & Rolfe, 2002). Gindhu & Schonert-Reichl (2005) state another gender difference – girls in their research only harmed themselves alone, while boys harmed themselves alone (71%), or with others (21%), or both (7%). Self-cutting was identified more frequently in girls (almost a half of the self-harming girls cut themselves, but only a third of the boys). Izutsu et al. (2006) describes the occurrence of self-hitting in 27.7% of boys and 12.2% of girls from 477 respondents at the average age of 14.19 years. However, we can see relatively more serious injuries in boys, which can sometimes result even in an accomplished suicide (Spender, 2007). Madge et al. (2008) also observed gender differences in the choice of form of self-harm – it was also proved here that girls cut themselves more often than boys (59.5% to 44.3%). In girls, self-poisoning is also probably more frequent when compared with boys (Harrington, 2001). Similarly, in a Belgian research study by Baetens et al. (2015) self-cutting was significantly more often observed in girls and head-banging in boys. According to Laukkanen et al. (2013), in adolescent self-cutters, girls more often than boys

---

50 Laukkanen et al. (2013) observed that the most common area for self-cutting is arms (in 67.2% of self-cutters). It seems that those who cut themselves in different areas than on the arms (32,8%) and chose rather hidden places on their bodies for self-cutting, more often have bigger emotional problems, dissociative symptoms and suicidal thoughts. At the same time, they also experience greater relief and feel better after cutting themselves than those who only cut themselves on their arms.

choose different areas for self-cutting than arms. In the Chinese research study by Wan et al. (2011), girls more often bit and cut themselves, whereas boys hit, pinched and burned themselves more frequently.

The research studies mapping the frequency of the used forms of self-harm come to ambiguous conclusions. Laye-Gindhu & Schonert-Reichl (2005) observed that 28% of girls and 13% of boys harmed themselves in more than one way. Three or four different forms of self-harm were used by 9% of girls. According to the research by Ross & Heath (2009), most of the self-harmers relatively significantly prefer and use one form of self-harm. Their research identified only 6.4% of self-harming individuals using more than one form of self-harm. Baetens et al. (2015) finds the use of only one form in 41.67% of self-harming Belgian adolescents. These realities are probably influenced by the fact that the mentioned studies do not sufficiently differentiate between adolescents with one-time experience, experimental experience, or long-term experience with self-harm.

2.7 The Influence of Developmental Changes on Self-Harm

The most significant trait of this developmental stage is physical maturation, progressing from sexual maturity[51] to mental, or psychological and social maturity. This process is realised through a number of substantial physical and mental changes, which also lead to fundamental personality changes in an adolescent individual and result in creating his or her adult identity (Blatný, 2010; Steensma et al., 2013; Sacks, 2014). According to most authors, developmental changes can be classified as biological, cognitive, emotional and psychosocial. Many of these changes happen primarily on the biological level, but they are also conditioned by many significant psychological and social factors, since the whole process of adolescence is also closely related to broader socio-cultural and economical conditions surrounding the individual, whose development progresses individually and is often asynchronous in particular areas of maturity. Therefore, it can be very difficult for adolescents to deal with individual important ongoing changes, especially if we consider the psychosocial significance which an individual ascribes to these changes and the way he/she experiences them (Schachter &

51 In simply organised communities, sexual maturity was recognised as a borderline between childhood and adulthood. The transition from childhood to adulthood was anchored through initiation rituals, which clearly determined when a young person became a full member of the group of adults. However, there was no intermediate phase which could be called adolescence. We can find similar rituals in native tribes even today.

Marschall, 2008). In the process of development in adolescence, one can identify several significant risk factors, which can co-influence the development of risky forms of behaviour and therefore also self-harm. Some of the most important ones are: imbalance between physical and mental and social maturity of an individual, imbalance between the social role and the status of an individual, imbalance between the values of an individual and the values of his or her family and the society as a whole.

Rissanen, Kylmä & Laukkanen (2008) in their qualitative research specified the main causes of self-harm in adolescents. They divided these causes into two basic categories – external and internal. The external causes include violence committed against the individual, fundamental life changes, overuse of drugs, interest in Satanism and similar movements, gaining information about manners of self-harm and also arguments between those close to the individual. The internal causes include unfair accusations, feelings of loneliness, important life changes, fear of violence, experience with an illness or with being different, low self-confidence and negative emotions. Undoubtedly, significant and sometimes abrupt physical, mental and social changes happen in this developmental period. Since an early start of these changes is accompanied by a rather high emotional strain and a number of negative feelings (e.g. a rather high level of tension and uncertainty), they can be, if they come too early, one of the risk factors in the development of various mental disorders (Hayward & Sanborn, 2002)[52] as well as this specific form of behaviour (Favazza, 1987; Hawton et al., 2002; Moran et al, 2012 and others). Early onset of developmental changes can also become a factor in other forms of risky behaviour, such as criminality, risky sexual behaviour, abuse of drugs, higher aggression, and others (Mrug, Hoza & Bukowski, 2008). Therefore, some specifics of this developmental period can, to a certain extent, contribute to a high prevalence of self-harming behaviour in adolescence, or to its massive development. In the context of a complex perspective on the phenomenon of self-harm in adolescence, we offer an elementary overview of the most significant changes which an adolescent individual goes through in this developmental period:

---

52 Hayward & Sanborn (2002) demonstrated the connection between adolescence and the development of panic disorder and eating disorders. They also demonstrated that adolescence is a stronger predictor of these disorders than chronological age. Klump (2013) summarises the conclusions of the research studies dealing with the connection between adolescence and the development of eating disorders, which highlight the fact that adolescence significantly increases the risk of eating disorder development.

Physical changes: the first signs of sexual maturity appear, conditioned by the change of hormonal functions (Spear, 2007)[53], and in most adolescents growth acceleration takes place, which can bring various difficulties with accepting physical changes[54] – it is in this period that possible discontent with physical appearance starts or deepens[55]. Since physical appearance is an essential part of identity of adolescents, its adequate acceptance is crucial. Due to negative social reactions especially of one's peers, physical adolescent development can be a significant source of stress, discontent with one's own body leading to a person losing respect for it, which subsequently facilitates self-harm (Muehlenkamp & Brausch, 2012). The development of risky forms of behaviour (and thus also self-harm) can be associated with secular acceleration[56], when adolescent individuals reach maturity in terms of physical and sexual growth earlier than they used to, which does not necessarily match their mental and social maturity (Rogol, Roemmich & Clark, 2002; Spear, 2007).

Maturation of cognitive processes: adolescent individuals are already capable of metacognition – the ability of reflecting on their own thinking is developing in them. The development of thinking allows them to change their perception and evaluation of the world around them, which is often associated with higher levels of criticism and egocentrism, manifested as oversensitivity (Feldman, 2004; Berzonsky, 2008; Kesselring & Muller, 2011). Adolescents are not very good at compromising, they tend to be radical, hypercritical and like to polemicize with others and identify themselves in terms of their perception of the world (Byrnes, 2008).

---

53 The body starts to secrete gonadotropic hormone in hypotalamus, which stimulates secretion of luteinizing and follicle-stimulating hormone in hypophysis (Sirotkin, 2005). These hormones further act on the organs of reproduction – they stimulate the production of testosterone in boys and estrogen in girls.

54 Each of these changes is sexually dimorphic – it is different for female and male gender (Rogol, Roemmich & Clark, 2002).

55 Macek (2003) adds in this context that, considering the pressures typical of our culture, earlier maturation is an advantage especially for well-equipped boys, in whom a significant physical growth and gain of muscles is visible at the first sight (Huan et al., 2007; Murray, Rieger & Byrne, 2013), which is also often connected with getting a higher social status. Based on the current demands of slenderness in girls (a socio-culturally determined ideal of beauty), they often reject the signs of physical maturity (Klump, 2013).

56 The age of the beginning of adolescence, defined from the biological point of view as the first menarche in women, lowered rapidly since the 19th and the beginning of the 20th century due to better nutrition, healthcare and living conditions in general (Euiling et al., 2008).

However, at the same time a new method of moral judgment gradually develops in them, so they are able to consider other people's opinions and behaviour and also look at themselves from other people's perspective, which helps them better observe and analyse their own thoughts and feelings. The development of cognitive skills subsequently leads to changes in understanding their own identity and allows for its formation.

Personality changes: in the period of adolescence, an overall change of parts of personality in an adolescent takes place through the processes of searching for one's identity, building one's self-image and self-esteem, and striving for a deeper understanding of the self, which is connected with the development of the ability of introspection. The significance of forming an identity lies in the necessity of perceiving oneself as a constant personality across various situations and contexts (Kroger, Martinussen & Marccia, 2010; Blatný, 2010; Hill et al., 2013). The development and achievement of such a personality is related to psychosocial maturity, which an adolescent individual is going through and which presupposes acquiring of such skills that would allow an individual to function independently and at the same time to interact with others within social norms (Koepke & Denissen, 2012)[57]. Another aspect formed in this period is self-esteem, which expresses the overall perceived value of an individual, or his or her attitude towards himself or herself (Richardson, Paxton & Thompson, 2009). The formation of self-esteem is influenced by a great number of important internal and external criteria, e.g. feedback from the closest social surroundings, achieved success and also the ability or, on the other hand, disability to deal with stressful situations. Negative self-evaluation can, therefore, even lead to the feelings of inability and worthlessness, which can be one of the reasons for the development of various risky forms of behaviour, including self-harm.

57 In the context of joining formal operations and forming of identity, Berzonsky (1999) distinguishes 3 styles which an adolescent can utilize to form his or her identity: informational (IS), normative (NS), and diffuse-avoidant (DA). In informational style, an individual searches for information relevant to his or her person, and processes and evaluates it. He or she is sceptical to his or her own view of the matter and his or her motivation is the perceived discrepancy between the personal ideal and the perceived feedback from his or her surroundings. An individual with NS automatically internalises standards and expectations of his or her surroundings. The discrepancy between the information about what he or she is like and about his or her normative standards brings the individual rather the feeling of guilt and fear of failure. An individual utilizing the DA style is associated with procrastination and the effort to avoid identity crises and fundamental decisions as long as possible.

Changes in emotional experience: biological changes in white and grey matter in the brain, or changes in neurotransmission of dopamine and extensive hormonal changes bring important emotional changes and instability (In-Albon, 2013b)[58]. Adolescent individuals have a tendency to overreact even to average stimuli, and they show impulsive behaviour as well as relatively violent emotional reactions inadequate to the situational context. Apart from emotional instability, various neurovegetative problems occur as a part of the process, e.g. sleeping disorders, appetite disorders, etc. In addition, feelings of tiredness and apathy often take turns with moments of heightened activity in them, which further helps to increase the feeling of emotional discomfort. Mood swings are very frequent, especially toward negative emotions, and violent swings of often extreme moods can lead to maladaptive ways of coping with them, e.g. through self-harm, which helps individuals to cope with excessive stress of the developmental period, but also with negative emotions, feelings of hopelessness, depressive moods, or anxiety (McLaughlin, Miller & Warwick, 1996). Emotions and self-regulation in general go through one of the most important developmental changes in this period – adolescents learn how to cope with them, control them and regulate their process. At the same time, in this period they also show a higher interest in seeking excitement, dangerous situations and even risky behaviour (Steinberg, 2005; Krettenauer et al., 2013). Consequently, we can consider the adolescent's experimentation with self-harm as a coping mechanism.

Change in interpersonal relationships: in the process of forming one's own identity, an adolescent is also building his or her social identity, which gradually gains significance during adolescence (Tanti et al., 2011). What can be considered very important in this context is a change in close relationships, which go through a rather violent development in adolescence from the individual izosexual phase – a close friendship with an individual of the same sex (Oerter & Montada, 2002) to the need of getting closer to an individual of the opposite sex – to the polygamous heterosexual phase, which can be a source of many conflicts and emotionally charged situations. Furthermore, it is also important to include possible troubles related to different sexual orientation. During the process of maturation, other close social relationships of adolescents change significantly as well – adolescents gradually move away from parental authority and turn to their peers as a source of solidarity and support (Kenny, Dooley & Fitzgerald, 2013). The influence of the relationship between an adolescent and his or her

58 These changes can be considered a part of a continuum in maturation on a hypothalamo-hypophyseal-gonadal axis (Fechner, 2002).

parents[59], whose quality along with the prevailing parental educational approach until then has significantly influenced the psychosocial development of the individual, gradually gets pushed into the background (Schachter & Ventura, 2008, Scheirer & Hansen, 2014). On the other hand, the quality of the relationship with peers, or the way an individual is integrated into the peer group and the level of his or her acceptance by others, gains importance[60], and adolescents engage in not only new but also in rather differentiated relationships (Collins & Steinberg, 2006). However, for a healthy transition of an adolescent individual into adulthood, a safe and supporting family environment[61] as well as that of the referential peer group is necessary (Viner et al., 2012), and the significance of peer group conformity is growing.

Adolescence is undoubtedly a crucial period for optimal integration of an individual into the society[62], and a badly socialised individual can engage in risky behaviour and activities which are not acceptable in the society (Garcia, Aluja & Barrio, 2006). Individuals, whose relationship with their parents and their peers is broken, show a higher risk of negative impact of such relationships, which includes states of anxiety and depression and many other negative influences, especially on their self-understanding (Raudino, Fergusson & Horwood, 2013). Such a person can try to cope with these negative influences using one of the maladaptive forms of behaviour (e.g. self-harm). On the other hand, satisfactory relationships with parents and peers are a significant protective factor preventing the development of risky forms of behaviour.

---

59 Note: or the primary carers.

60 Adolescents can engage in behaviour which is risky if they can use this behaviour to prove their value for the group in the eyes of their peers (it can be various adrenalin sports or even more dangerous criminal activities (Javdani, Sadeh & Verona, 2011).

61 Adolescents learn how to communicate, solve conflicts, regulate themselves and also their emotions in the family (Scharf & Mayseless, 2008) and those who feel that the relationship with their parents satisfy their emotional and physical needs develop such an internal representation of themselves and others which they would perceive as safe (Raudino, Fergusson & Horwood, 2013).

62 A well socialised individual is conformist, sociable, emphatic and emotionally affectionate, on the other hand, a badly socialised individual is characterised as stubborn, indifferent, uninvolved, unsocial, emotionally reserved and unable to respond to social stimuli by appropriate behaviour and emotions (Garcia, Aluja & Barrio, 2006).

3 Risk and Protective Factors of Self-Harm

Self-harm behaviour is viewed by the majority of society and in most cultures as socially unacceptable and typically serves the idiosyncratic purpose of coping with a personal problem or subjective distress (Claes & Vandereycken, 2007). Self-harm behaviour can be broadly categorised as including both direct and indirect modes of self-damaging acts such as NSSI, suicide attempts and particular eating, drinking and smoking habits (Lloyd-Richardson et al., 2007; St. Germain & Holley, 2012). Considering the closeness of the terms "self-harm" and "self-injury", we can base the main areas, which can be risky for the development of self-harm, on the Biopsychosocial Model for Self-Injury, as described by Heath & Nixon (2009).

Figure 7. Biopsychosocial model for self-injury (Heath & Nixon, 2009, p. 146).

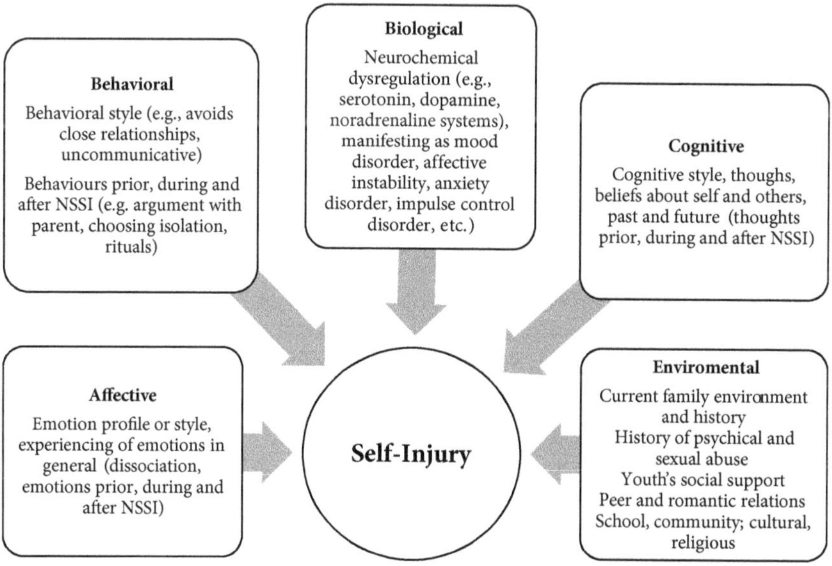

The combination of these influences, along with the various degrees of their intensity, is highly individual in each person. It follows from the above-mentioned model that these crucial areas can also fulfil the protective function at the other end of the risk continuum. Risk factors condition the increase of the likelihood of negative outcome. In this case, these are conditions that precede and directly or indirectly contribute to the onset and maintenance of NSSI (Whitlock & Selekman, 2014). Protective factors are conditions that effectively buffer adolescents from a negative outcome. The same as risk factors, protective factors may precede or co-occur with self-harm behaviour and may directly or indirectly influence the development or continuation of this risky form of behaviour.

Individual level risk factors can have a very varied image – however, if self-harm occurs and develops, some of these factors function in a relatively large measure in most self-harming individuals. Apart from female gender and adolescent age, they include impulsiveness, difficulties with sexual identity, low social support, social isolation, being a part of a specific sub-culture (gothic, emo), family problems, or previous suicide attempts (Spender, 2007; Mustanski & Liu, 2013). Based on their studies of the results of current research in the given area, Klonsky & Glenn (2009) list the following familiar basic psychological risk categories:

1. emotion dysregulation (e.g. negative emotionality, dissociate experiences, alexithymia),
2. self-derogation, childhood adversity (e.g. attachment difficulties, familial neglect, child abuse), and
3. comorbid or antecedent psychiatric disorders (e.g. anxiety, depression, eating disorders, substance abuse).

Subsequently, Hawton, Saunders & O'Connor (2012) in their study list the risk factors of self-harm also common for suicidal behaviour, which can be found in works of other authors as well (Fergusson, Woodward & Horwood, 2000; Hulten et al., 2001 – for more details see chapter 2.2.). For the purpose of this publication, a basic overview of risk/protective biological and personality factors is briefly described further on, and the role of family and peer group as well as broader socio-economic influences are mapped, since the combinations of many biological, psychological and social factors often contribute to the development of self-harming behaviour (Veague, 2008). It is also necessary to acknowledge the fact that it is not always simple to distinguish the meaning of individual risk factors, nor is it easy to specify the exact degree of their influence on the final occurrence and possibly also the development of self-harming behaviour[63].

63 Author's note: for example, as a result of inadequate early developmental conditions (deprivation, neglect, traumatising family environment, etc.), the biological and personality parts of an adolescent individual develop in a different manner than they would otherwise have, if he/she had been growing up in a sufficiently saturating environment.

3.1 Biological Factors

These factors have been partially described in the chapter about etiology of self-harm, and apart from neurological dysregulation, e.g. serotonin, noradrenalin and dopamine systems manifesting as mood disorder, affective instability, anxiety disorder and impulse control disorder, etc. (Osuch, Payne, 2009; Favazza, 2011[64]), professional literature also very often describes some significant hereditary influences[65] as well as, for example, gender differences in the occurrence of this phenomena.

The above-mentioned neurological dysregulation can be either congenital or acquired – e.g. a lower level of serotonin often occurs in adults who suffered from malnutrition or abuse in their childhood (Nock, 2009), and a research hypothesis has been successfully verified that individuals who were sexually and otherwise abused as children habituated to high concentrations of endogenous opiates in their childhood (as a result of the violence they experienced) and in the moments of stress they subsequently show higher pain threshold and need high concentrations of these drugs to cope with stress (Skegg, 2005).

It is possible to trace hereditary proneness to anxiety, depressive tendencies, impulsiveness, and low resilience to stress in many self-harming individuals. It then depends on the broader conditions of their development if self-harm develops as a result of this proneness (Levenkron, 2006; Groschwitz & Plener, 2012). In some individuals who self-harm over a long period of time, even certain genetic anomalies[66] or genetic polymorphism[67] were found, which probably causes the changed sensitivity to pain and the emotional reaction to such pain (Nock, 2009)[68].

---

64 Favazza in this publication states that if there is an excessive amount of dopamine in the brain, especially in the nucleus caudatus, anxiety, irritability and uneasiness increase, which can sometimes lead to self-harm, which diminishes such unpleasant feelings. Similarly, anxiety and depressive tendencies grow if there is not enough serotonin or non-adrenalin in the brain. A certain role is probably also played by the hormones of the hypothalamic–pituitary–adrenal axis.

65 Research studies identified genetic conditionality of self-harm and recorded a higher risk of self-harm in individuals in the families where a suicide occurred, and a higher concentration of self-harm is in identical twins when compared to a control group of fraternal twins (Skegg, 2005).

66 It is a reduplication of the long arm of chromosome 22 along with the inversion on this chromosome (Nock, 2009).

67 It is a polymorphism of the catechol-O-methyl transferase, which is also located on chromosome 22 (Nock, 2009).

68 Caspi et al. (2003) found that functional gene polymorphism for serotonin transporter influences the impact of stressful events on the development and risk of suicidal behaviour.

A great number of research studies also describe a gender difference in the occurrence of self-harm, and the most frequently stated ratio of its occurrence is 2–3:1 with the predominance of girls (Portzky, De Wilde & van Heeringen, 2007; Hargus et al., 2009; Madge et al., 2011; Moran et al., 2012 and others.). However, if authors of research studies include drinking alcohol and smoking tobacco in the definition of self-harm, boys show 1–2 times higher frequency of self-harm (Izutsu et al., 2006). Rozsívalová, Trefilová & Paclt (2010) claim that in Czech conditions the ratio of girls to boys in early adolescence is 8:1 and in middle adolescence 3:1. Subsequently, Burešová & Hrubá (2012) identified the ratio 3:2 in a group of 12–16 year-old adolescents[69]. Hawton, Saunders & O'Connor (2012) in this context point to the fact that boys probably have more natural opportunities to release tension and aggression, and list interesting connections concerning the development of the occurrence of self-harm in relation to gender in a lifetime.[70] Spender (2007) also claims that more girls self-harm than boys, this trend getting more balanced with rising age. Gender differences can also be found in the preferred manners of self-harm (Van Camp, Desmet & Verhaeghe, 2011; Ciuhodaru, Iorga & Romedea, 2012), and if we examine the motives leading to self-harm, according to Lloyd-Richardson et al. (2007), we can more often find motives that could be marked as social in boys, while in girls these are rather interpersonal reasons (see chapter 2.5 and 2.6). Whitlock (2010) is also convinced that there is a gender difference in the motives of this risky form of behaviour and in the preferred manners of self-harm (men choose more self-hitting or various blows to the body, while women choose more scratching and cutting themselves), as well as in the seriousness of this behaviour[71]. Nevertheless, in accordance with the conclusions of Baetens et al., Whitlock (2013) finds the assumption about higher self-harm in women faulty, since he sees the probability of its occurrence as well as its development as the same for both sexes.

69 The differences in results stated in the studies are also given by differing methods of carried out research as well as the differences in terminology, or differences in the content of the term self-harm in individual studies.

70 The author claims that in early adolescence there are more self-harming girls than boys, and the peak of the occurrence of self-harm in girls is in the period between 15–24 years, while in men in the period of 20–35 years.

71 Madge et al. (2008) state that boys were hospitalised due to a self-harming episode twice more often. Sutton (2005) in this context claims that in boys, socially more acceptable coping strategies for dealing with emotional problems were evolved, for example drinking alcohol and fights. Boys also release their tension physically in aggressive sports more often (Sutton, 2005).

3.2 Personality Factors

Concerning factors which play a significant role in the occurrence and development of self-harm and simultaneously in connection with personality[72], professional literature most often references the connection with anxiety and depressive tendencies (Moran et al., 2012; Beatens et al., 2013; Dir, Karyadi & Cyders, 2013; Tormoen et al., 2013 and others[73]), or impulsiveness (Madge et al., 2011; Di Pierro et al., 2012; Dir, Karyadi & Cyders, 2013; Yusainy & Lawrence, 2014 and others[74]). The important role of hostility is also very often stated (Ross & Heath, 2002) and another significant factor mentioned is alexithymia (Paivio & McCulloch, 2004; Evren & Evren, 2005; Sutton, 2007; Hsu et al, 2013 and others). This inability to cognitively process emotions is a relatively stable personality trait, which is more frequent in depressive and anxious individuals (Honkalampi et al., 2004; Zimmermann et al., 2005; Karukivi et al., 2010; Tolmunen et al., 2011 and others)[75], who have problems with recognising and describing their emotions as well as emotions of other people. In these individuals there is a risk of being flooded with strong and nameless emotions, or memories (Sutton, 2007). However, as they are not able to describe or share these experiences, they seek release through self-harm (Veague, 2008)[76].

In his research, Brown (2009) mapped the personality traits from the Big Five Model, and the biggest difference between the group of subjects who self-harmed and the group who did not was found in neuroticism, which was significantly higher in self-harming individuals – the author assumes that this fact

---

72 For more details, see Chapter 2.3.

73 Compare in older research studies, e.g.: Harrington, 2001; Ross & Heath, 2002; Sutton, 2005; Tick et al., 2008; Brausch & Gutierrez, 2009, 2010; Gunter et al., 2011; Wan et al., 2011.

74 See also Mangall & Jurkovich (2008), Glenn & Klonsky (2010), Carli et al. (2010), Evren et al. (2010) and Gunter et al. (2011).

75 Alexithymia also increases vulnerability to psychosomatic illnesses (for example in mental anorexia – see Parling, Mortazavi & Ghader, 2010). Research studies show that behavioural and physiological impact of alexithymia can be one of the causes of illnesses, like post traumatic stress syndrome, depression, drug abuse, anxiety disorders and somatoform disorders (e.g. Meganck et al., 2009; Lumley, Neely & Burger, 2010; Carlstedt, 2010; Williams, Curren & Bruce, 2011).

76 Some other frequent traits of individuals with alexithymia are: lack of sympathy, poor introspection and insight, cold and evasive interpersonal style with frequent problems in relationships, maladaptive emotion regulation, tendency to somatisation and external locus of control (Veague, 2008).

points to their predisposition to experience negative emotions as anxiety, anger, or depression. According to In-Albon (2013b), in some self-harmers, a higher emotional reactivity and over-sensitivity was found, in others, on the other hand, a lower ability to realise one's own feelings. McMahon et al. (2013) in this context highlight the important connection between coping strategies, mental health and self-harm. Favazza (2011) describes in self-harmers a higher proneness to injuries, weakened ability to solve problems and limited stress coping strategies, along with frequent dissatisfaction with their sexual orientation as well as their own body, which has been verified by the conclusions of other authors (e.g. Wan et al., 2011; Muehlenkamp & Brausch, 2012; Dakanalis et al., 2013), who describe the link between the occurrence of self-harm and the way self-harmers experience their body image. Subsequently, Madge et al. (2011) state a higher risk of the occurrence of self-harm in young homosexuals and bisexuals, who are still not sure about their sexual identity.

Levenkron in his study (2006) describes the personal characteristic of self-harming individuals in the following manner: these are individuals who are often emotionally fragile, highly sensitive to refusal, and whose mental balance can be easily undermined. They often have problems with starting new relationships due to distrust, frequently suffer from the feelings of helplessness, loneliness and anger, feel different from others and easily become outsiders. A similar characteristic of self-harming individuals, who often have low self-confidence and suffer from a negative self-image and self-hatred, is also presented by Sutton (2007). However, the author highlights the fact that these individuals are often also perfectionists and very successful in some areas, but their school results are often unstable due to emotional lability (Levenkron, 2006). Danchin et al. (2010) connect the occurrence of self-harm with inadequate demands on oneself, while Yusainy and Lawrence (2014) with the level of self-control. A great number of personal traits and characteristics can therefore contribute to the occurrence and development of self-harm, but very individually and to various degrees. In non-clinical population of adolescents, the results of the European comparative study CASE, which proved the correlation between self-harm and anxiety, depressive tendencies, impulsiveness and low self-esteem, can be considered crucial. With the growing level of depressive tendencies, anxiety, impulsiveness and decreasing self-esteem, adolescents more often self-harmed repeatedly (Madge et al., 2011). In this context, Brausch & Gutierrez (2010) highlight the important role of the level of self-esteem, projecting itself into the broader conditions of the life of an adolescent in relation to protective factors guarding him/her against the development of this risky behaviour.

3.3 Family Influence

The level of self-esteem in the developmental stage of adolescence is built upon especially the quality of the closest social relationships of the adolescent individual, which are realised primarily in the environment of the family, and with the rising age, peer groups also become more and more important. Brausch & Gutierrez (see above) highlight its significant role, which, along with the adequate support of the close social environment, fulfils the role of a safety barrier protecting against the development of this risky form of behaviour. In the study carried out by the authors, parental support also influenced whether adolescents only self-harmed or whether they had suicidal attempts in their personal history as well.

Many authors have explored the connection between the applied educational styles[77], or subjectively perceived parental support, and the occurrence of self-harm (Muehlenkamp & Gutierrez, 2004; Sutton, 2007; Polk and Liss, 2007; Klimusová, Burešová & Bartošová, 2013[78]). Miller, Rathus & Linehan (2007, p. 106) brought interesting conclusions describing two extreme parental educational styles, which can contribute to the development of self-harm and between which the authors of the study recommend finding a balance: showing too much indulgence and not giving enough rules versus having authoritarian attitude and giving too many rules; worrying too little and not taking the problems in the child's behaviour seriously enough versus worrying too much and taking the problems in the child's behaviour too seriously; not being protective enough and giving too much freedom to the child versus being overprotective and not giving enough freedom to the child.

Nevertheless, self-harming adolescents claim to have mostly negative relationships with their parents or primary care givers, and most often these are uncertain or traumatic attachment relationships[79] (Hsu et al., 2013), separation and the experience of a loss in childhood, poor quality of relationships in the

---

77 Polk and Liss (2007) state that self-harmers could have lacked emotional saturation in their personal history, which, along with the authoritative parental style and strict rules, predicated self-harming behaviour in subjects from their research file.

78 The authors of this study claim that adolescents with experimental and especially repeated experience with self-harm perceive the relationships with both parents as substantially worse than the control group of subjects without their own experience with self-harm.

79 Hallab & Covic (2010) learned that respondents who self-harmed had a weaker attachment to both parents, which, according to the authors of the study, could have led to the development of maladaptive forms of coping with negative emotions and stress.

family, or excessive parental criticism (Wedig & Nock, 2007; Kenny, Dooley & Fitzgerald, 2013). Di Pierro et al. (2012) in their research proved a connection between a negative relationship with the mother and both the occurrence of self-harm and its seriousness, while the relationship with the father (characterised by poor communication, rare displays of affection and high degree of admiration and imitation) influenced the seriousness of this behaviour[80]. Adrian and his colleagues (2011) point to the direct influence of family relations on self-harm, or inadequate development of emotionality, which predicts the development of self-harm. The authors postulate that there is a connection between emotional imbalance and self-harm without the intention to die, which is developed by unsupportive social context – it is the emotional balance that is a crucial characteristic of self-harm, and problems in the family and with peers have a significant influence on the occurrence as well as the progress of self-harm. In this context, Baetens and her colleagues (2015) state that the lack of emotional support from one's parents is directly connected with the occurrence of self-harming behaviour, and also even indirectly increases the risk of self-harm through the influence on the occurrence of depressive moods in adolescents. According to the authors of the study, excessive parental criticism probably also influences the occurrence of self-harm through a higher degree of self-criticism in this developmental period, which is critical for the development of risky forms of behaviour.

The occurrence and especially the development of self-harm can significantly influence a wider range of conditions in which an adolescent grows up. The roots of the particularly more serious forms of self-harm are often found especially in social isolation in childhood[81], or in a childhood trauma (Harrington, 2001; Mazelis, 2008), which can be caused by a great number of stressful life situations, for example: a loss of a significant person, most often a parent (death, divorce, or

---

If a child lacks safe family environment, he/she does not create a proper relationship with his/her body, which can be manifested even by auto-aggressive behaviour.

80 The authors in this context highlight the importance of strong discrepancy between a real and an ideal father-child relationship.

81 Social isolation in early childhood predisposes one to a lack of social competencies, inability to adapt to changes, frustration, depressive tendencies and developmental retardation. This can subsequently lead to self-harming behaviour, which was proved in humans as well as in animals. Other risk factors are the experience of having surgeries or a stay in a hospital in early childhood, alcoholism or depression in parents, a refusal by a significant person and the helplessness, anger or guilt that follow (Favazza, 2011).

long separation), neglect[82], child abuse or sexual abuse[83], exposure to violence in the family, or even strong imbalance in power relationships in the family system.

An important role is played by the presence of mental illness in parents, or their addiction to drugs, the occurrence of self-harm in parents[84], substitute family care, or institutional care, taking over a parental role by a child, and many other factors (Suton, 2007). Portzky, de Wilde & van Heeringen (2007) claim that the risk of self-harming behaviour increases with the occurrence of serious life events in the previous year (in exceptional cases even earlier), and these are most often arguments with parents, friends, and partners, suicidal attempts, or a completed suicide of a close person, and worries related to sexual orientation[85]. Madge at al. (2011) in this context state that individuals who have a great number of stressful life events in their personal history self-harm more frequently and more seriously. The results by Sutton (2007), who observed the occurrence of these events in personal histories of self-harmers, are very significant in this context: 14% of them were sexually abused in their childhood, 33% were emotionally or mentally abused, 11% were neglected, 62% lost a close person, 54% were battered, 47% were bullied, 31% did not have good experience with relationships, 34% of them were raped. Frequently, there was a combination of several of these events and only 14% of the self-harming respondents claimed that they had a happy childhood.

Laye-Gindhu and Schonert-Reichl (2005) confirm even more frequent occurrence of self-harm in adolescents from incomplete families (in individuals who grew up in a single-parent family, or in a family with a parent and his/her new partner), and similar conclusions were also presented by Kvermo and Rosenvinge (2009). Similarly, a more frequent occurrence of self-harm was found in

82 Lieberman (2004) states that, compared to the control group, self-harming individuals more often come from divorced families or from families where neglect, lack of parental care and acceptance occurred.

83 For example: Murray et al. (2008) explored the connection between sexual abuse in childhood and higher risk of self-harm. Apart from sexual abuse in childhood, which has the closest connection with subsequent self-harm, other forms of self-harm appeared, like emotional blackmail, emotional neglect, physical abuse and physical neglect.

84 For example, Hargus, Hawton Rodham. (2009), and McMahon et al. (2010) state that the occurrence of self-harming behaviour in the family increases the risk of self-harm in other family members. Therefore, we can regard social imitation as a theoretical principle of transmission of self-harming behaviour.

85 The above stated events increased the risk of self-harming behaviour if they did not happen earlier than in the previous year. The exception was a suicide of a parent or a close friend, where an influence of events which happened earlier than a year ago was found.

individuals who have four or more siblings (Meltzer et al., 2001) and many research studies illustrate a connection between the occurrence of self-harm and family status (Wan et al., 2011). The support of the quality of family attachments and family cohesion, therefore, gains an important place in preventive, intervention, therapeutic and treatment programmes focusing on self-harm (for more details see Chapter 6), since the importance of family and its influence on harmonic or disharmonic development of a child cannot be questioned.

3.4 The Influence of Peer Groups

The significance of peer groups and their influence on adolescents increases along with gradual diminishing of the influence of family, parents, or primary carers in the process of one's individual progress of development and maturation. Hargus, Hawton and Rodham (2009) claim that usually up to 80% of adolescents state that they know at least one peer in their surroundings who harms himself/herself. In their own research study, 73% of self-harming girls and 57% of self-harming boys stated that they are friends with somebody who also harms himself/herself. Also, the results of a study by Burešová & Klimusová (2014) carried out on a large non-clinical sample of adolescents conclude that self-harmers most frequently (in 67% of cases) confide in their peers concerning their behaviour. At the same time, from the above-mentioned research sample, the repetitive self-harmers claimed that they spend about 5 hours per week more hanging out with their friends. This finding conflicts with the idea of a self-harmer as a loner and socially isolated individual. On the contrary, it implies that self-harmers have a tendency to strengthen peer relationships and that they share their experience with this risky form of behaviour.

Peer groups can function as a highly protective[86] as well as risky factor in the occurrence and development of self-harm and they can encourage an adolescent to experiment with various risky forms of behaviour (smoking, drug abuse including alcohol, risky sexual and delinquent behaviour, etc.). If an individual has a friend, or a group of friends, who engage in such behaviour, this fact becomes a significant predictor of the probability of occurrence of risky behaviour in the individual (Weiss & Baker-Smith, 2007). Dyl (2008) draws attention to the existence of school groups, where cutting oneself is a condition for membership. Being accepted by peers depends on other qualities and conditions than being accepted by one's family. Adolescents who want to belong to a certain group

86 A substantial protective factor against suicidal thoughts and the development of self-harming behaviour lies in e.g. team sports (Dugas et al., 2012).

usually must prove their "attractiveness" for other members of the group, which happens through manifestation of certain skills, abilities, or qualifications. If they cannot attract members of the group by different (more adaptable) means, they may search for other ways of attracting this group due to their need to be accepted, and it is in this situation that an opportunity arises to demonstrate risky forms of behaviour (Hawton et al., 2002; Raudino, Fergusson & Horwood, 2013). Already Suyemoto (1998) has stated, in this context, that for a certain number of self-harming individuals in a social group the attention and social status gained from the peer group (as a result of the demonstrated ability to bear pain) is a means of strong consolidation of self-harming behaviour. What can also be significant for the development of self-harm in adolescence is the influence of various subcultures[87], e.g. Emo-style, Gothic and other, which are associated not only with a certain make-up and hair style and typical styles of clothing and music, but also with self-harm and suicidal attempts. Another important role is played here by an easy access to information about self-harm via the internet and the subsequent imitation of this behaviour by disposed individuals, or individuals undergoing a crisis (Mitchell & Ybarra, 2007) because self-harming behaviour has the tendency to occur in clusters, since it easily leads to imitation.

Nevertheless, the development of self-harming behaviour in adolescents, meaning the transition from experimenting with this highly risky form of behaviour to its more frequent use, is usually preceded by a significant negative event (long-term or short-term) in their lives, or an intense stress impetus, which is (after problems in the family and arguing with parents) most often a break-up with a boyfriend/girlfriend, problems in partner and peer relationships, or problems at school (Harrington et al., 2001; Cooper et al., 2006; McMahon et al., 2010). The adolescent period is particularly stressful in regards to interpersonal issues, more specifically the impact of peer influence and peer victimization including online bullying (Nixon et al., 2015). As stated above, adolescents whose present personal history involves a great number of stressful life situations, or a current combination thereof, self-harm more seriously and more often, and the reasons (apart from troubles in family relationships) are most often problems in relationships with peers, exclusion from a peer group, experience of bullying, bad school results, problems in school performance, conflicts with teachers, etc. (Evren, Evren, 2005; McMahon et al., 2010; Madge at al., 2011).

---

87 Distinctive minority groups within the culture of the majority. Subcultures of adolescents have an essential place in the process of socialization. Especially in the period of adolescence, peer groups become a unique and irreplaceable educational factor due to their dynamics.

The influence of social environment on the occurrence and development of self-harm is very significant – in a negative as well as positive way – because good close relationships with one's family and friends (characterised especially by open communication, expressed support and experienced feelings of acceptance), stable partner relationship and the overall experience of social support diminishes the risk of self-harm in people who face highly stressful life situations, or current stress (Evans, Hawton, Rodham, 2004; Skegg, 2005). However, creating good relationships with peers in itself does not ensure protection against self-harm (Fergusson, Woodward & Horwood, 2000). Despite the specifics of the adolescent period, these relationships are still generally of lesser importance to adolescent individuals in life crisis situations than the feeling of support from their primary family (Brausch & Gutierrez, 2010).

3.5 Socio-Economic Influences and the Impact of Mass Media and Social Networks

The development of each individual is, in an important manner, influenced and formed by a broader social context in which it takes place. It involves especially the prevailing values, norms, habits, and moral or religious norms given by the society and its culture (Krettenauer et al., 2013), or current political problems of the society, but also other significant socio-economic influences. In the context of the occurrence of self-harming behaviour in non-clinical population in adolescence, a number of such influences, which could be somehow connected with its development, have been researched. The research studies carried out in this area aim mostly at socio-cultural factors connected with nationality, key socio-economical influences, the importance of religion or participation in religious life, and the significance of the impact of mass media and social networks.

The results of up-to-date research, which are based on the comparison between self-harm in this age category in various countries and are further described in chapter 2.1., highlight particularly the influence of socio-cultural factors connected with nationality (González-Forteza et al., 2005; Portzky, De Wilde & van Heeringen, 2007; Wan et al., 2011; Swahn et al., 2012; Tormoen et al., 2013; Coughlan et al., 2014; Baetens et al., 2015 and others). The difference between the frequency of occurrence of self-harm in relation to nationality is also documented in the results of the above-mentioned extensive European comparative study CASE (Madge et al., 2008). Similarly, for example in the USA Ougrin et al. (2012) describe a higher occurrence of self-harming behaviour in Hispanic girls and in Native Americans compared to the rest of the American population. The occurrence of self-harm, therefore, apparently relatively significantly varies between cultures, which can be also explained (apart from many other intervening influences) by the different value systems of the cultures, or their attitude to one's body and self-harm (e.g. in connection with certain rites of passage in the development of an individual, or as a part of religious rituals related to a given faith). Very low occurrence of self-harming behaviour in some Catholic and Islamic countries can be linked to religion, which strictly condemns any form of self-harm, thoughts of ending one's life and suicide as a sin. Strong religious traditions in such countries can play a protective role against the development of self-harm[88], but on the other hand, they can also lead to a strong inner conflict and thus put an individual under pressure, which results in finding a solution in a hidden form of this risky behaviour[89] (Malone et al., 2000; Dervic et al., 2004).

Significant socio-economic factors, which are usually connected with the occurrence and development of self-harm, are reflected especially in its broader social psychological causes, meaning the consequences of general social changes, or individual specific burdens (low socio-economic family status, the loss of its social standing most often related to the loss of employment of both parents, or for whatever reason considerably worsened economic situation of the family, low education of the parents, social exclusion of the family for being of different race or religion or being migrants, and other reasons). The occurrence of self-harm is not limited to a certain socio-economical group, but the risk of its occurrence and subsequent development shows in many respects a parallel identical with the development of other forms of risky behaviour in the period of adolescence – it is higher in adolescents who come from dysfunctional families and from families undergoing a crisis (Fletcher, Steinberg & Williams-Wheeler, 2004; Skegg, 2005; DiClemente, Santelli & Crosby, 2009; Tan, Rehfuss, Suarez & Parks-Savage, 2012).

From the group of factors which can contribute to the development of risky behaviour in adolescents at the level of broader socio-economical environment, Hawkins et al. (2000) further mention significant aspects related to broader conditions of a local community and highlight some concrete predictors in this context, such as poverty, disorganisation of the local community, or an individual repeatedly facing violence and racial prejudice. Furthermore, the importance of certain social groups in which self-harm is not only tolerated, but even frequently admired,

88 The protective role of religion, membership in a religious organization, and participation in religious life are usually used in preventive and systematic treatment strategies focused on prevention and treatment of self-harm (author's note).

89 In this case, a major role is played by moral conflict resulting from the teachings of the particular religion, and self-harm is in these cases connected with a deep feeling of guilt (Statham, Heath & Madden, 1998).

e.g. the Emo or Gothic subcultures[90] should not be omitted. Despite the fact that the influence of such subcultures is recently diminishing, Hrubá et al. (2012) in their recent research identified their members among self-harmers in the group of participants with their own, single or repeated, experience with self-harm.

Broader socio-economical conditions of each society are reflected in the manner its adolescents use their free time, or in the opportunities a particular individual has – one of the triggers of interest in self-harm could possibly be the feeling of boredom and the lack of meaningful free-time activities. Watching media and sharing information on social networks[91], which play an important role in raising awareness of self-harm, belong to everyday free-time activities of a great number of adolescents. The scale of media information about self-harm was addressed by e.g. Purington & Whitlock (2010)[92], who, with regard to the fact that until the 80s of the 20th century mentioning self-harm in the media was rare, put the increase of the prevalence of self-harming behaviour in context with a more frequent media presentation of this phenomena. In their view, its presentation in media can show self-harming behaviour as one of the regular coping strategies and it can therefore be perceived as common, which can further support its spreading. Transue and Whitlock (2010) point out in this context that adolescents usually perceive media as something which sets the trends, not as something which could negatively influence them.

Therefore, in case of self-harm it is possible that media provide a distorted view of the issue, and thus strengthen the stereotypes, which are closely connected to this form of behaviour among adolescents, or even introduce individuals,

---

90 In the Emo subculture, whose name is derived from the word emotional, the ability to express one's emotional state (especially in case of negative feelings) and possibly release one's "life suffering" through self-harm is highly valued. Similarly, the members of the Gothic subculture are known for their interest in darkness and blackness, which is close to death and is demonstrated on the outside in their specific style of clothing and make-up as well as in the overall image – self-harm can bring the sensations of a close death.

91 Rheingold (2010) in the context of social networks claims that the status of social networks on the scale of values of today's adolescents is so high that they have become a part and parcel of the life of almost every adolescent, influencing them fundamentally in many ways.

92 The authors state that at the time of creating their contribution, it was possible to find over 15 million hits and more than 2000 videos online related to the subject of self-harm, and they referred to studies which proved a strong influence of media for example on accepting fashion trends, quitting smoking, suicides or eating disorders.

who have had no prior information about it, to this specific form of behaviour[93]. The information about self-harm presented through media and social networks[94] is therefore often partial and distorted, which can inspire immature individuals to gain their own experience with such behaviour[95]. The importance of media and social networks in the context of the development of self-harm is thus based on the fact that adolescent individuals perceive them primarily as setting trends, which entails all the above-mentioned risks.

---

93 The current media presentation of self-harm contains a high number of references, which are related to this form of behaviour. These are various web pages, discussion forums and blogs on social networks, which connect self-harmers, or those who want to know more about this risky form of behaviour. Furthermore, many works of art are being created, which are spread through mass media and in which self-harm often occurs connected with strong and, for an adolescent individual, significant contents. From today's and in a way also mainstream artists, we can mention for example the singer Pink, who shot a video Fuckin Perfect in 2010 where the main heroine harms herself with a razor, which is framed by her desire to be perfect; the longing to half-poison oneself in order to get closer to death is presented by the song Burn by the band We Are the Fallen (2010), etc.

94 Social networks (like e.g. Facebook, Twitter, Instagram, Badoo and others) in publicly available internet environment are currently the fastest spreading social phenomenon. In general, one can describe them as applications which enable people to start and maintain social relationships with others, communicate with individual members, help with presenting the personality of the user, group, or organisation in virtual environment, share the contents of individual user profiles in which various contributions, opinions, commentaries, notifications of oncoming events, photos, etc. become public, and if the user allows it, also personal data – which all helps to maintain and develop the particular virtual community.

95 In the area of media and cultural studies, which are concerned with the given issues, a clear agreement on the influence of media on human behaviour has not been reached. In research studies on this topic, two main groups of hypotheses can be identified: the first one is usually described as reflection hypothesis (Renzetti and Curran, 2005) and its basis is the assumption that media only reflect reality, i.e. reflect and present what happens in the society. The second theory assumes that media and the pictures which they present form and construct certain patterns and models, which become a part of an individual's reality.

4 Lexical Trace of the Term Self-Harm in Adolescents

This chapter contributes to the explanation of how self-harm is perceived by adolescents themselves, since it presents sub-conclusions of an extensive project called Verifying Psychometric Qualities of Diagnostic Tools for Screening of Occurrence and Forms of Self-Harm in Adolescence. This research was carried out in the Czech Republic in the years 2011 and 2012 and its key results have already been presented at several places in this publication (Burešová, Klimusová, 2014; Burešová, Bartošová & Čerňák, 2015; Burešová, Vrbová & Čerňák, 2015; Hrubá, Burešová & Čerňák, 2015; etc.).

As a part of the above-mentioned project an exploration research substudy was carried out, focused on mapping the perception of self-harm in adolescents from non-clinical population. Its key research aim was to trace possible differences in the way self-harm is perceived by adolescent individuals in relation to their experience with self-harm and gender. We find the analysis of the lexical trace of this term crucial, since this area still remains completely unexplored, allowing for an insight into the understanding of the phenomena through an adolescent's eyes.

The research sample consisted of 3164 respondents (48% boys, 52% girls) between 12 and 16 years of age (m = 13.98). Considering the above-mentioned aim, we have chosen a combination of quantitative and qualitative design, carried out primarily through linguistic text analysis of the answers of respondents freely answering the question of what they themselves perceive as self-harm. Subsequently, they were divided into three compared groups: without their own experience with self-harm, with a vicarious experience of self-harm and with personal experience with this behaviour.

The subjects participating in the research project completed an extensive battery of measures. In the present study, we summarize data concerning the subjects' age and sex and partial data from the Self-Harm Inventory (Sansone, Wiederman, Sansone, 1998) and Self-Harm Behaviour Questionnaire (Gutierrez et al., 2001). After splitting the research file into three groups according to the stated experience with self-harm, the data was processed through quantitative linguistic text analysis, which for the purpose of this study was carried out in three steps:

1) Lemmatization – when tokens (individual words) were transferred to lemmas, which is the basic form of each word (e.g. tokens "razors" and "razored" were transformed into the basic form "razor"). This is related to disambiguation, or decisions concerning the basic form in case of ambiguity. What helps the researcher to decide which of the basic forms of the word is generated is the consideration of the base of a particular word as well as the neighbouring words. Also, the QUITA software was used and POS tagging (marking the token as corresponding to a particular type of speech) was carried out.
2) Division of texts into groups based on gender and experience with self-harm – based on this division, these groups were subsequently compared with each other.
3) Computation of indexes and creation of tables of frequency wise interesting autosemantic words, which allows for ordering the obtained lemmas according to the frequency of occurrence and helps to define a point above which mostly synsemantic words (without their own meaning) occur and below which occur autosemantic lemmas, which have meaning on their own[96].

The open-ended responses of the respondents to the question "What do I consider self-harm" contained 34804 tokens, out of which 3071 unique lemmas were obtained through lemmatization[97]. The activity index was 0.75, which shows that activity significantly dominated over description in these responses.

As far as types of speech are concerned, nouns were used most frequently (27.2%), then pronouns (22.2%) and verbs (16.3%), which is captured in Figure 8, which also depicts the types of speech of the most frequently used words in the whole research file.

---

96 This line can be determined on the basis of the h-point, which is a place where the order of the word equals its frequency. The lexical trace is formed by autosemantic words which are above the set line, in other words, in the synsemantic area. These autosemantic words have a frequency, which is higher than the frequency expected in the average population and show us the author's focus on a certain topic. The lexical trace is closely connected with the thematic concentration index (TC for the h-point and STC for the 2h-point), which is normalised to the scale of 0–1. The second index, which we identified in the given groups of individuals, is the textual activity/descriptiveness index. This index expresses the relationship between types of speech which we use when describing something, e.g. nouns, adjectives (A) and the type of speech expressing an activity, i.e. verbs (V). This relation is given by the following formula: A/(A+V), or V/(A+V) (Čech, Popescu & Altmann, 2014; Haviger, Havigerová & Loudová, 2015).

97 The h-point for this file is 77 and the defining line formed by the 2h-point is 154. Among 154 of the most frequent lemmas, there are 84 autosemantic words with a frequency higher than 154. The index of thematic concentration of the text for the 2h-point is 0.023.

Figure 8. The use of autosemantic words in the whole research file. Adjectives are blue, nouns are orange and verbs are red.

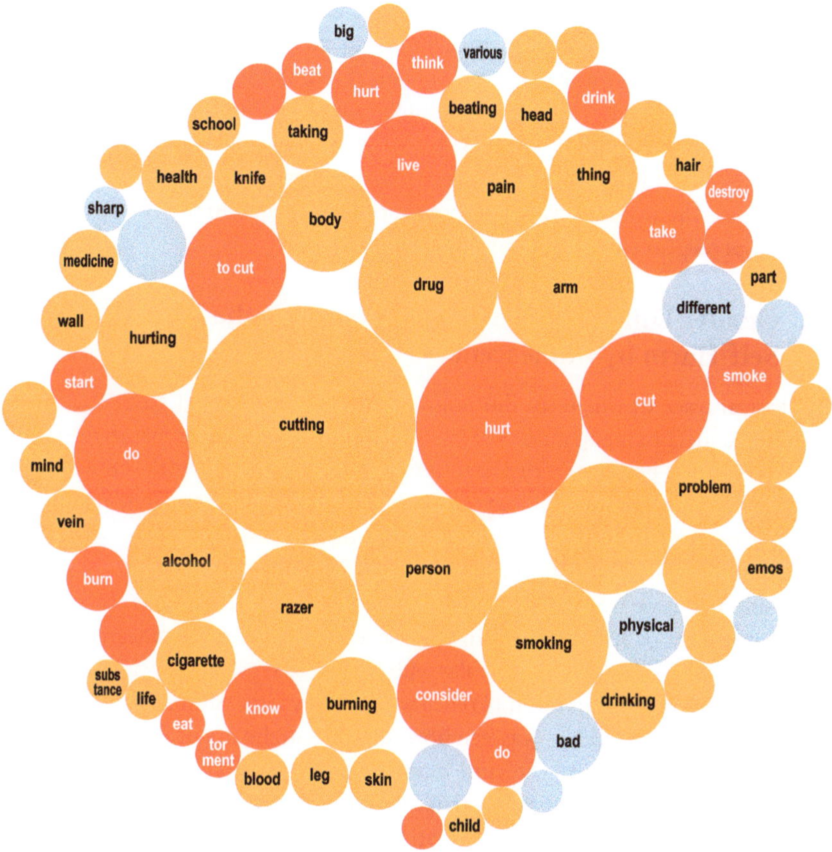

The first ten lemmas used were the following: *cutting, hurt, person, drug, arm, cut, self-harm, smoking, razor and alcohol*[98]. From the perspective of the interpretation, within the whole file of respondents the idea of self-harm therefore appears primarily as self-cutting (*cutting, cut, razor*) and drug abuse (*drugs, alcohol, smoking*).

98 The lemma *cut* was an imperative, the frequency of which contributes to the otherwise most frequent lemma cutting, occurring most often in adolescents with their own and repeated experience with self-harm in the form of a compulsive urge to act.

It was also revealed that for adolescents self-harm is most often connected with upper extremities (*arm*). There is another interesting word at the 13th position – *cut* – which also supports the most frequent concept of self-harm. At the 16th position is the word *pain*, which points to the conception of self-harm as something causing pain (as opposed to drugs), but it could also be the perception of self-harm as a tool for diminishing pain[99]. At the 18th position was the word *burning* as a different type of skin damage and at the 23rd position was the word *cigarette*, which can be connected with both burning and drugs. At the 31st position was the word *suicide*, which supports its meaning in the context of adolescents' perception of self-harming behaviour.

4.1 Gender Differences in the Perception of the Term Self-Harm by Adolescents

The lexical trace of this term did not differ much in boys and girls. They used a similar conceptual apparatus, which is also illustrated by the fact that 91% of lemmas used by boys were identical to those used by girls. In girls, 68% of lemmas were identical to those in boys. This was given by a higher number of girls in the research file and thus by a higher number of detected lemmas.

The thematic concentration index was slightly higher in boys, which could be the result of a more frequent use of autosemantic words than in girls. The activity index was more or less the same in both sexes (activity was significantly higher than description). The case was similar with the use of types of speech – boys used nouns more than girls but this difference was not very large. Similarly, it turned out that there was no difference between boys and girls in the use of the word *suicide*, which was stated by almost the same number of girls (0.26%) as boys (0.27%).

However, one interesting fact is that out of the recorded words, boys used the following additional words: *beat*, *own* and *doing drugs*; and girls used the following additional words: *problem*, *burn*, *think*, *skin*, *medicine*, *mind*, *pill*, *lighter*, *blood* and *overdose*. Also, the understanding of self-harm as drug-abuse was more frequent in boys. However, the words related to taking drugs and drug overdose did not occur in boys – it is therefore an area which is specific for the understanding of the term in girls. A slight difference occurred also in the perception of self-harm as being physical (this type was more frequently stated by boys), or as mental (which was more often stated by girls). The results are illustrated by Figure 9 and 10.

99 This interpretation also applies to subsequent text.

Figure 9. The relation of the order of words in boys and girls. The y axis shows the order according to the frequency of words in boys and the rule is that the higher the word, the higher its position and the lower its frequency. The x axis shows the order according to the frequency of words in girls and the rule is that the more to the right a word is, the higher its position and the lower its frequency. It follows that the words with higher frequency are under the axis in boys and the words with higher frequency are above the axis in girls (e.g. the word smoke is typical for boys since it is on the 45th position, while for girls it is on the 83rd position). Blue colour represents adjectives, orange nouns and red verbs.

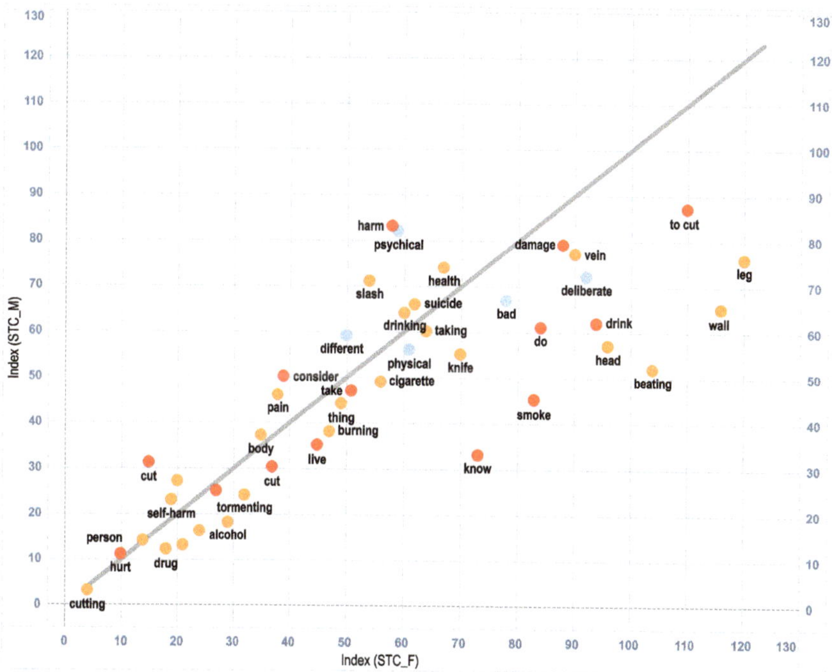

Figure 10. Comparison of the most frequently occurring words in both sexes. On the left – girls, on the right – boys; categories are sorted by frequency in boys.

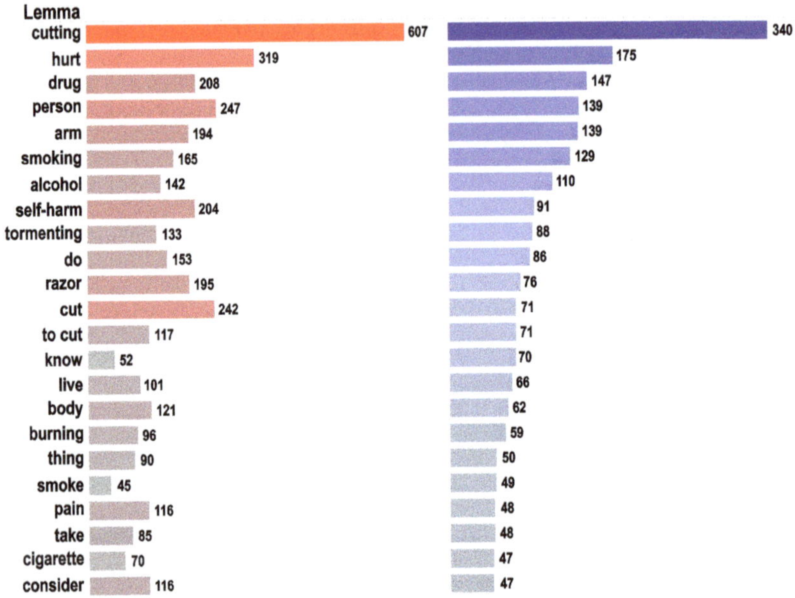

4.2 Understanding of Self-Harm in Adolescents Based on their Experience with Self-Harm

The open-ended responses of the adolescents who did not have any experience with self-harm contained 10433 tokens, out of which 1484 unique lemmas were obtained through lemmatization[100]. The first ten lemmas used were: *cutting, hurt, person, drug, arm, self-harm, smoking, do, alcohol* and *self-harm*. At the 11th position was the lemma *cut*[101]. The term self-harm was mostly connected with upper extremities (*arm*) in this group of subjects. Other interesting words were *cut*

100 As far as types of speech are concerned, the most frequent were nouns (25.7%), pronouns (22.7%) and verbs (17.3%). The h-point for this file of lemmas is 44.6 and the defining line set by the 2h-point is 89. Among the 89 of the most frequent lemmas, there are 48 autosemantic words with a frequency higher than 89. Thematic concentration index of the text for the 2h-point is 0.026. The activity index is 0.75, which shows that activity significantly predominates over description in these responses.

101 Similarly to other groups of subjects, the word *cut* was used here as an imperative – as an emotionally charged compulsive urge to a self-harming act.

at the 15th position and *pain* at the 20th position. The word at the 22nd position was *burning* as a different kind of skin damage, and at the 26th position was the word *cigarette*, which can be related to burning as well as drugs. At the 28th position was the word *suicide*. From the perspective of interpretation, the idea of self-harm, therefore, appears to be primarily cutting (*cutting*) and drug abuse (*drug, alcohol* and *smoking*).

The open-ended responses of the adolescents with vicarious experience with self-harm contained 15890 tokens, out of which 1817 lemmas were obtained through lemmatization[102]. The first ten lemmas used were almost the same: *cutting, hurt, drug, cut, person, razor, arm, smoking, self-harm* and *alcohol*, but in a different order according to the rate of frequency. Also, in this group of subjects, the term self-harm was mostly related to upper extremities (*arm*). Another interesting word was the lemma *cut* at the 13th position as well as the word *pain* at the 15th position. At the 19th position was the word *burning* as a different type of skin damage and at the 22nd position was the word *cigarette* – these lemmas occurred more often than it was common in the respondents without personal experience with self-harm. At the 31st position was the word *suicide*. From the perspective of interpretation, the idea of self-harm is again mainly cutting (*cutting, razor*) and drug abuse (*drug, alcohol,* and *smoking*).

The open-ended responses of the adolescents who claimed their own experience with self-harm contained 8481 tokens, out of which 1397 unique lemmas were obtained through lemmatization[103]. The first ten lemmas used were: *cutting, person, arm, harm, razor, self-harm, drug, cut, smoking* and *alcohol*. Also, among these subjects, self-harm was most commonly connected with upper extremities (*arm*). Another interesting word was *burning* as a different type of skin damage at the 12th position. Afterwards, the word *pain* followed at the 14th position, the word *cut* at

102 As far as types of speech are concerned, the most frequent were nouns (26.8%), pronouns (22.5%) and verbs (16.2%). The h-point for this file of lemmas is 53.6 and the defining line set by the 2h-point is 107. Among the 107 most frequent lemmas, there are 56 autosemantic words with a frequency higher than 107. The thematic concentration index of the text for the 2h-point is 0.028. The activity index is 0.75, which shows that activity significantly dominates over description in these responses.

103 As far as types of speech are concerned, the most common were nouns (29.4%), pronouns (20.6%) and verbs (15%). The h-point for this file of lemmas is 41 and the defining line set by the 2h-point is 82. Among the 82 most frequent lemmas, there are 43 autosemantic words with a frequency higher than 82. The thematic concentration index of the text for the 2h-point is 0.033. The activity index is 0.71, which shows that activity significantly predominates over description in these responses.

the 16th position, which again supports the most common conception of self-harm, and the word *cigarette* at the 27th position. The word *suicide* was only at the 37th position, which supports the theoretical concept of an act of self-harm as protection against suicidal behaviour (more details in Chap. 1.2.). From the perspective of interpretation, in this group of subjects the idea of self-harm is again mainly connected with cutting (*cutting, razor*) and the use of drugs (*drug, alcohol* and *smoking*).

All the respondents used a similar conceptual apparatus to describe this term, which is illustrated by the fact that 95% of the lemmas detected in individuals with personal experience with self-harm were identical with those in individuals with vicarious experience with this behaviour. Also, 86% of the lemmas detected in individuals with personal experience with self-harm were identical with those in individuals without such personal experience. The lexical trace in the respondents with various extent of experience with self-harm did not differ in any extreme way. However, it was possible to find some very interesting discrepancies in the results – especially the differing frequency in the use of some words and also the differences in the occurrence of some words.

Some of the detected words occurred relatively often in the individuals with personal experience with self-harm, e.g. the word *leg*, which reflects a different location of self-harm than is the commonly perceived one. Individuals with vicarious experience of self-harm used the following additional words: *emo, subject, school, harass, big* and *start*. Individuals without personal experience with self-harm used the following words significantly more often: *overdose, cut*, and *beat*, which reflects the qualitative differences in the perception of this term by individual groups of subjects. In individuals who claimed to have personal experience with self-harm, the understanding of self-harm as drug abuse occurred less frequently when compared with other groups. On the other hand, this conception of self-harm occurred most often in the group with vicarious experience with self-harm.

The use of the word *suicide* showed that it was used the least by individuals with personal experience with self-harm and by the individuals with vicarious experience with this behaviour (0.24% in both), while individuals without experience with self-harm used the word more often (0.31%). The word which occurred significantly more frequently in the adolescents who had personal experience with self-harm was "mental", while the word "physical" was the most frequent in respondents without this experience. Also, the thematic concentration index was higher in individuals with personal experience with self-harm, which may reflect a more frequent usage of autosemantic words in this group of subjects, compared to individuals with vicarious or no experience. This finding could be used when constructing a specialised tool for detection of individuals at risk of this form of behaviour employed, for example, in prevention and intervention programmes at schools.

5 Diagnostic Tools Used in Research and Clinical Practice

There are various reasons why mental health professionals and scientists might want to measure adolescent self-harm. The diagnostic tools, used in the developmental stage of adolescence to identify the prevalence of self-harm, its frequency or its forms in both clinical and research practice, are built upon a variety of methodological bases – most often upon tracing the occurrence and subsequent behaviour description. These tools include primarily self-assessment scales as well as scales based on which the behaviour is assessed by an individual close to or caring for the adolescent, a pedagogue, healthcare personnel,, a psychiatrist or a psychologist).

Most of these methods provide the respondents with a list of several most frequent forms of self-harm, and the respondent's state if they have personally used any of the given options, or they can even add an option not offered on the given list (Latimer, Meade & Tennat, 2013). The occurrence of self-harm is commonly traced either for the period of the last year, the last 6 months, or the last month prior to gathering research or clinical data, or for the period of an individual's lifetime (i.e. life-long prevalence). Within this framework, the methods focused on identifying self-harm also try to trace the frequency of occurrence of this behaviour and possibly also the forms of self-harm used by the respondents (e.g. cutting, burning, torturing oneself by thoughts of one's own suffering etc.). Some methods also concentrate on the individual's motivation for this risky behaviour, or they aim to trace the presence of suicidal tendencies. It is also common to map other important realities, e.g. if the respondent had to seek medical help, which helps to assess the seriousness of the injury, or under what specific conditions an individual carried out this behaviour and how he or she felt before and after the self-harming act.

In theoretical perspective, methods for classifying self-harm are usually divided into those which focus on self-harm without the intention to die (non-suicidal self-injury) and those which include suicide (deliberate self-harm). The following Table 6 summarises and illustrates the selection of the most frequently employed methods, which were created after the year 1990[104] and which fulfil the minimum criteria for psychometric adequacy.

104 Some of these methods are not designed primarily for the developmental stage of adolescence, but with minor adjustments they are commonly employed for this period in practice.

Table 6. A brief selection of methods for identifying self-harm in research and in practice

Title *Author, year*	Brief method description
Child Behaviour Checklist[a] *Achenbach, 1991*	The method includes 120 items and it is employed to identify problematic behaviour in general. The items are completed by a person who is close to the child/adolescent – most often a parent or a teacher. The number of items focusing on self-harm is relatively small.
Self-Injury Survey *Simpson, 1994*	The method has a four-page, self-report measure with 31 self-harm items, a write-in listing of suicide attempts, and a check-off list of reasons for self-injury, types of past interventions, and damage effects. This measure explores suicidal ideation as well.
Self-Harm Inventory (SHI)[b] *Sansone, Sansone & Wiederman, 1995*	The inventory uses 22 items to capture the forms and frequency of possible self-harming behaviour, and respondents first indicate whether they have ever carried out the particular form of behaviour, and subsequently, if they claimed to have personal experience, they also state the number of repetitions. Apart from the common forms of self-harm (like cutting, burning, or preventing the healing of wounds), the method also includes e.g. deliberately withdrawing from God as a form of self-punishment, dropping out of school or deliberately losing a job. The advantage of this method is that it is not time-consuming and is also suitable for screening.
Impulsive and Self-Harm Questionnaire (ISHQ) *Rossotto, 1997*	It is a 14-item, one-page, self-report survey with Likert-style response options that explores a variety of impulsive and self-destructive behaviours (e.g., self-mutilation, accident proneness), including suicide attempts. This measure was developed for a dissertation and has had limited clinical exposure.
Self-Injury Inventory *Zlotnick et al., 1996*	The method observes self-destructive and impulsive acts and self-mutilative acts without intent to die. It maps frequency, duration and types of self-injury.
Self-Injury Questionnaire (SIQ)[c] *Vanderlinden & Van-dereycken, 1997*	Self-assessment survey designed specially and only for examining deliberate self-harm. The method uses 54 items to map the frequency, type, function and duration of self-harm, but also affective stimuli and the consequences of such behaviour. SIQ has many forms together with a great diversity in meanings. In order to develop an individually tailored treatment plan, the primary diagnostic task is to pinpoint the behaviour and its current developmental process, i.e. identifying the external (e.g. reduced social attention) and internal (e.g. anxiety, anger) stimulus conditions that contribute directly to the instigation of SIQ. Hence, a treatment-related assessment seeks to determine the motives, purposes or functions of SIQ.

Title *Author, year*	Brief method description
Functional Assessment of Self-Mutilation (FASM)[d] *Lloyd, Kelley & Hope, 1997*	The method consists of two parts – in the first part, respondents' mark which of the 11 offered forms of self-harm they carried out in the last twelve months. They also state the frequency of this behaviour, how long this episode lasted and whether they had to seek medical help. The forms of self-harm are divided into two categories: 1) serious (cutting oneself, burning oneself, the so-called rubbing – the use of an eraser to rub the skin to such an extent that it results in burning or bleeding, and other) and 2) minor (inserting objects under nails or skin, preventing the healing of wounds, pulling one's hair, etc.). As regards forms of self-harm, the method also offers the option of an open-ended response. The second part includes 22 statements, which describe the motivation for self-harm. Respondents choose options from a 4-point Likert scale. The use of this survey is desirable in adolescents aged 13–18 years.
Self-Injury Questionnaire (SIQ) *Alexander, 1999*	The method observes body alternations (e.g., piercing), indirect self-harm, failure to care for oneself and overt self-injury. It maps frequency, types and reasons for self-injury.
Self-harm Behaviour Questionnaire (SHBQ) *Guttierez, Osman, Barriors & Kopper, 2001*	The survey includes 4 sub-scales related to self-harming behaviour, suicidal attempts, threats to commit suicide and suicidal ideas. It is a combination of items with a constrained choice and open-ended responses. As opposed to other surveys, it measures the entire life period, and it stresses mainly the last experience with self-harm. It does not offer any pre-selected forms of self-harm or suicidal attempts. The respondent is incited to an independent description and the obtained information is subsequently processed qualitatively. The advantage is that it is a relatively low time-consuming method combined with a relatively objective way of interpreting the responses. It is also suitable for non-clinical population.
Deliberate Self-Harm Inventory (DSHI)[e] *Gratz, 2001*	The inventory offers 17 forms of self-harm, where the respondent chooses whether he or she has or has not had personal experience with these forms – this method focuses only on the forms which result in tissue damage. It also examines the time when the respondent started and finished with self-harm and whether he or she had to seek medical help due to this form of behaviour. The inventory deliberately excludes questions about risky behaviour which is not physically self-harming – e.g. promiscuity.

Title *Author, year*	Brief method description
Ottawa Self-Injury Inventory *Nixon & Cloutier, 2002*	The method concentrates on suicidal ideation and suicidal attempts and a method identifies of this behaviour, its frequency, reasons, context, addictive properties, the effect of this behaviour on regulating negative affect and motivation for change.
Self-Injury Self-Report Inventory (SISRI) *Juzwin, 2004*	Apart from deliberate self-harm, the self-assessment survey also observes suicidal behaviour, eating disorders, drug abuse and the history of traumatic events.
Ottawa Self-Injury Inventory (OSI)[f] *Cloutier & Nixon, 2005*	The method uses 21 items to examine self-harming behaviour and thinking patterns without the intention to die over a period of the last month and the preceding six months. It identifies the frequency of suicidal thoughts in the last year and life-long occurrence of failed suicide attempts. It maps detailed information about the forms of self-harm and motivation. Respondents also state when it first occurred to them to self-harm, if they told anyone about the fact that they harm themselves and if they had to seek medical help after any of the self-harming episodes. Apart from the given options, in most items there is also the possibility of an open-ended response, where the respondents are encouraged to describe their experience if it does not match any of the offered categories. The method is used for respondents aged 14–18 years and it is designed directly for self-harming individuals – it can also be used for screening. The outcome of this method is a detailed description of experience with self-harming behaviour, the possible therapy and motivation for therapy. The obvious disadvantage of the method is the fact that it is time-consuming.
Self-Injurious Thoughts and Behaviours Inventory (SITBI)[g] *Nock, Holmberg, Photos, Michel, 2007*	The SITBI is a structured interview that assesses the presence, frequency, and characteristics of a wide range of self-injurious thoughts and behaviours, including suicidal ideation, suicide plans, suicide gestures, suicide attempts, and non-suicidal self-injury. The method can be used as a structured interview and also as a self-assessment survey.
Adolescent Risk Inventory *Lescano et al., 2007*	It is a two-page, 33-item, self-report inventory, with mostly yes/no response options that explores high-risk behaviours and attitudes. While a majority of items relate to high-risk sexual behaviours, six items explore self-harm behaviour including self-cutting and suicide attempts.

Title *Author, year*	Brief method description
Inventory of Statements About Self-injury (ISAS) *Klonsky & Glenn, 2009*	The survey is used with younger adults, but it can also be used in the developmental stage of late adolescence. It maps 13 possible functions of self-harm and focuses on inner as well as outer reasons and the frequency of self-harming behaviour.
Self-Harm Quest. (SHQ) *Ougrin & Boege, 2013*	The Self Harm Questionnaire (SHQ) aims at identifying self-harm in adolescents and it is very good at helping to predict future episodes of self-harm.

Note. [a] The method was used in several research studies, e.g. Lam (2009 in Muehlenkamp et al. 2012), Hasking et al. (2010). [b] The method was used for example by Claes, et al. 2010, 1012; Gordon, et al. 2012 and others. [c] The method was used for example by Santa Mina et al. (2006). [d] The method was used e.g. in the research studies by Yates (2004), Lloyd et al. (2007), Hankin (2010 in Muehlenkamp et al. 2012), Tan et al., 2012, Zetterqvist, Lundh & Svedin (2012) and others. [e] It was used e.g. in the research by Lundh, Karim & Quilisch (2007) or Cerutti et al. (2011). [f] The method was used in their research by e.g. Plener et al. (2005, 2009), Bureau et al. (2010). [g] The method was referred to by e.g. Nock et al., 2007, or Muehlenkamp, Walsh & McDade, 2010.

Self-harming behaviour can also be discovered by using more complex tools, such as the very frequently utilised diagnostic interview Kiddie-Sads-Present and Lifetime Version (K-SADS-PL, Coughlan et al., 2014). For many reasons, the methods of this type seem more advantageous for identifying self-harm and its individual causes, symptoms, progress and motivations, especially considering the possibility of a subsequent individually tailored treatment (therapy) plan (Cloutier & Humphreys, 2009).

In their publication on the measurement of non-suicidal self-injury in adolescents, Cloutier & Humphreys (2008, p. 115) in this context state: "Although self-report measures do bring the risk of response biases (e.g., social desirability), such biases might be reduced with the use of structured interviews, which also hold the advantage of being systematic and objective models of gathering information." As opposed to the case of research on self-harm, in clinical practice clinical assessment, treatment planning and monitoring, and evidence-based practice are used more.

6 Preventive Strategy and Therapeutic Approaches

Self-harm is common in adolescence, but most young people who self-harm do not seek professional help – between a third and one half of adolescents who self-harm do not seek help for this behaviour (Rowe et al., 2014). Of those who seek help, results showed adolescents primarily turned to friends (Hrubá, Klimusová & Burešová, 2012) and family for support, or they ask a pedagogue for help or advice. Considering these facts, it is necessary to show heightened attention to the occurrence of self-harm in adolescence both at home and in schools (Ougrin & Zundel, 2009; Miller & Brock, 2010), and a broad range of helping professionals should be informed about its symptoms – school advisers, psychologists, etopedists, pedagogues, etc.

Lieberman (2004) in his theoretical study lists some typical traits, which can lead to the suspicion of self-harm in an individual:

- numerous inexplicable scars (cut wounds and burns), most often located on arms, thighs or belly, or even fractures (fingers, arms, wrists, toes);
- possession of sharp objects (razors, needles);
- continuous wearing of clothes which allow to hide scars (long sleeves, skirts and trousers), reluctance to undress in front of other people as a part of the preparation for PE classes or regular medical check-ups;
- spending unusually long time in the bathroom, or in other isolated places, secretiveness;
- significant symptoms of depression, social and emotional isolation, abuse of addictive drugs;
- extreme fear, sadness, pain, or signalling of physical harm during classroom work, or other creative activities;
- extremely dangerous behaviour which can lead to injuries.

6.1 Preventive Strategies Focused on Self-Harm in Adolescence

With regard to multifactorial aetiology of self-harm and the number of risk factors, which are projected with various levels of intensity into its highly individual image in each person, it is necessary to penetrate into the background of this highly risky behaviour and subsequently approach its prevention and treatment in as complex way as possible. Primary and secondary prevention should therefore concentrate not only on raising public awareness of the symptoms and consequences of such behaviour, but also on the support of mental health and healthy lifestyle of adolescents in general.

According to Ougrin et al. (2012), preventive programs for adolescents focusing on self-harm clearly raise awareness of self-harm in adolescents, but on the other hand, it has not been credibly proven that they also diminish the risk of self-harm. This fact can be due to inadequacy of the chosen methods, forms and means through which preventive programmes are implemented, or it can be the consequence of the aetiology of the behaviour itself, because of its multifactorial cause and the fact that its development is influenced by a number of inner and outer influences, which preventive measures cannot possibly cover completely.

The design of preventive strategies and programmes should encompass as much of the complexity of this behaviour as possible, ideally through the so-called peer programmes, including the simulations of dealing with stressful situations and the development of self-regulation mechanisms, since poor emotion regulation skills along with higher levels of emotional reactivity may be a risk factor for engagement in self-harm (Crawford et al., 2003; Nock & Prinstein, 2004). In addition, these programmes should examine and work with the values and the meaning of life of adolescents in this both crucial and risky phase of their development, and should focus on searching for and reinforcing sources of their inner happiness – ideally with the help and intensive engagement of their broader social surroundings.

According to Muehlenkamp, Walsh & McDade (2010), the educational programme The Signs of Self-Injury Program (SOSI), which includes an educational module for school employees and a module for students, seems potentially suitable for the above-mentioned task. Tan et al. (2012) find it useful, in terms of prevention, to implement programmes and procedures for adolescents focused on coping with stress and processing one's emotions. The authors, in addition, find it important to raise awareness of the issues related to self-harm among broader non-professional public in contact with adolescents – especially pedagogues and parents. This approach to prevention of the development of self-harm, based on research results, is also recommended by McMahon et al. (2013), who state that the development of positive coping strategies and the support of coping with emotions can be an appropriate way to prevent thoughts of self-harm as well as self-harm itself.

6.2 Treatment and Therapeutic Approaches to Self-Harm in Adolescence

There are a great number of treatment (therapeutic) approaches to self-harm, but they all agree on the fact that treatment must always be based on positive attitudes toward the self-injurer and proceed via a detailed individual formulation.

The choice of therapy is determined by the underlying causes of the behaviour (Duffy, 2006). The treatment goals for self-harming adolescents include: managing underlying psychiatric disorders, identifying triggers for self-harm acts, improving family relationships and developing better communication and coping skills. It usually also focuses on improving affective language skills, acquiring frustration tolerance, and learning alternatives to self-injury, which are the key to strengthening coping abilities. It addresses problem-solving skills because self-harming adolescents often lack these abilities.

Every treatment or therapeutic programme should start with a very detailed analysis of the causes, symptoms and consequences of self-harm, and it is necessary to aim at getting as complex information as possible about the start, the causes of development and the mechanisms of sustaining such behaviour, both from the self-harmer and his/her closest social surroundings (see the previous chapter – Nock et al., 2007; 2008). The procedure of this process according to Peterson, Feedenthal & Coles (2010) is illustrated in Table 7.

Table 7. Strategies for assessing adolescent self-harm (Peterson, Feedenthal & Coles, 2010)

Complete a thorough psychiatric evaluation.
Interview the adolescent separately from parents.
Obtain collateral information from parents and family, teachers, caseworkers, and others as needed.
Use an empathic, non-judgmental manner.
Note appearance and presence of scarring and bruises, and patient's clothing style.
Ask about current and past self-harming thoughts and behaviour: ▪ suicidal thoughts: frequency, duration, plans, and any triggers ▪ suicide intent: extent of desire to carry out suicidal thoughts and die ▪ past suicide attempts: number of attempts, methods, intentions, and consequences ▪ non-suicidal self-injury: total episodes, duration, frequency, and triggers for self-harm
Ask about acute stressors (e.g., break-up, loss or rejection, conflict with parents).
Inquire about thoughts, feelings, and events leading up to the self-harm episode.
Assess for psychosis and ask about homicidal thoughts. If yes, assess whether there is a duty to warn others.
Ask about drug/alcohol use and consider a urine toxicology screen to help clarify whether substance abuse problems may be contributing to self-harm. Assess family interaction and communication style, noting conflicts that might impact safety. Consider using a standardized measure, such as the Scale for Suicidal Ideation (Holi et al., 2005).

The subsequent treatment of self-harm can be very varied because its indication depends on a specific combination of many individual internal and external conditions affecting the development of this behaviour, the seriousness of self-harm, the duration of its occurrence and possibly psychiatric comorbidity. One of the most important basic building stones of a treatment approach, which to a certain extent also affects its result, is the quality of the relationship between the client and the therapist, on which depend all the corresponding procedures and processes from the already mentioned analysis to the broadest possible context of internal and external conditions of self-harm in the individual. Every therapeutic relationship focused on self-harm should include, apart from creating the therapeutic relationship, a functional analysis of the client's behaviour, and subsequently clearly defined procedures, which would lead to the change of cognitive and conative processes (Butler, 2012).

The most frequently used tool of complex treatment approach to self-harm is individual and group therapy, very often also supplemented by family therapy, or relaxation techniques[105,106], and in indicated cases of psychiatric comorbidity with other disorders also by pharmacotherapy (Simon, 2006; Bridge et al., 2007; Klonsky et al., 2011). The aim of the therapy for self-harm is primarily to protect the individual who carries out this highly risky form of behaviour – thus reduce the number of self-harming episodes, achieve a reduction of the craving to harm oneself, improve the functioning of the individual in the society, and raise the quality of his/her life in general, but, above all, to prevent some possible forms of self-injury which could be more serious, as well as suicidal attempts (Lilley & Owens, 2009; Peterson, Feedenthal & Coles, 2010; Asarnow et al., 2011; Butler, 2012; Ougrin

105 There are many psychotherapeutic movements focusing on the treatment of self-harm – cognitive behavioural therapy and similar movements are frequently used (e.g. the KBT focused on trauma, Dialectical Behavioural Therapy, Integrative Cognitive Therapy, and Multimodal Cognitive-Behavioural Approach). Also the movements like Narrative Approach by Dusty Miller, Rational Emotive Therapy by A. Elise, or Therapy focused on problem-solving (Tyrer et al., 2003; Townsend et al., 2001).

106 Some other employed therapeutic approaches described in professional literature up to the year 2010 are stated in an overview study by Ougrin et al. (2012). This overview includes e.g. interventions focused on problem-solving and increasing engagement, cognitive behavioural approaches focused on problem solving and self-direction, family home therapy with the help of social workers, dialectical behavioural therapy, developmental group psychotherapy, psychodynamic group psychotherapy, individual cognitive analytic therapy focused on the prevention of borderline personality development, family therapy based on attachment, therapeutic system for self-harm, group training of working with emotions and other.

et al., 2015 and others). As a part of short therapy, Ougrin et al. (2012) recommends working according to the Cognitive Analytic Therapy Model:

- The first step is a classical anamnesis of the individual's psychosocial history and the assessment of risks;
- subsequently, together with the self-harming individual, a diagram is created, which shows the cycle of self-harm, the so called vicious circle sustaining self-harming behaviour;
- then follows the identification of the targeted problem and searching and reinforcing the motivation for change;
- another step is searching for means to break the vicious circle of self-harming behaviour, the so-called stepping out of the vicious circle;
- finally, the whole diagram of self-harming behaviour is described again including the agreed-upon means of stepping out of the vicious circle.

McConnell & Lewis (2007) point to the fact that in the treatment approach to self-harm many clinicians rely on no-harm contracts or agreements; nevertheless, there is no evidence that they are effective[107]. Many writers also highlight the fact that psychosocial treatments for suicidal behaviours and self-harm are similar because with both, the priority is to help the patient maintain safety (Lewis, 2007). Peterson, Feedenthal & Coles (2010, p. 24) in this context state that: "…for non-suicidal self-injury this may include: developing a collaborative safety plan with family, increasing monitoring, removing access to firearms or other lethal means, helping the adolescent to develop alternate, safer coping methods". According to Asarnow et al. (2011), as a part of the treatment approach to self-harm, it is therefore possible to also use an empirically verified crisis intervention called Family Intervention for Suicide Prevention (FISP), which is based on cognitive behavioural therapy. This approach includes: psychoeducation; reinforcement of the family function and support of healthy communication; emotions, triggers and physiological signals "thermometer"; creating a safety plan with coping strategies for dealing with emotions through behavioural and cognitive strategies, and practicing the steps used in coping with acute stress.

---

107 Although suicide is a rare occurrence, clinicians face assessment of clients' risk for harming themselves on a regular basis. One well-accepted and widely practiced intervention for suicidal ideation is the use of no-harm contracts (NHC), but the existing research does not support the use of such contracts as a method for preventing suicide, neither in case of self-harming clients nor for protecting clinicians from malpractice litigation in the event of a client suicide (McConnell & Lewis, 2007).

Reviewing thoughts and feelings leading up to a self-harm act is sometimes very difficult, but it is crucial for the effectiveness of the treatment procedure because it can help identify triggers, coping difficulties, and issues to address during treatment. This behavioural analysis can be completed using the mnemonic ABC (Peterson, Feedenthal & Coles, 2010, p. 23):

- Antecedents (situations or stressors leading to self-harming thoughts or actions)
- Behaviour characteristics (frequency, intensity, and duration of self-harming)
- Consequences (e.g, emotional relief, care and attention from others).

Also, the systematic approach to self-harm designed by Heath & Nixon (2009), which is very much suitable for practice, can be considered very beneficial in this context (clearly described in Figure 11).

Figure 11. Hierarchical step approach to assessment (Heath & Nixon, 2009, p. 145).

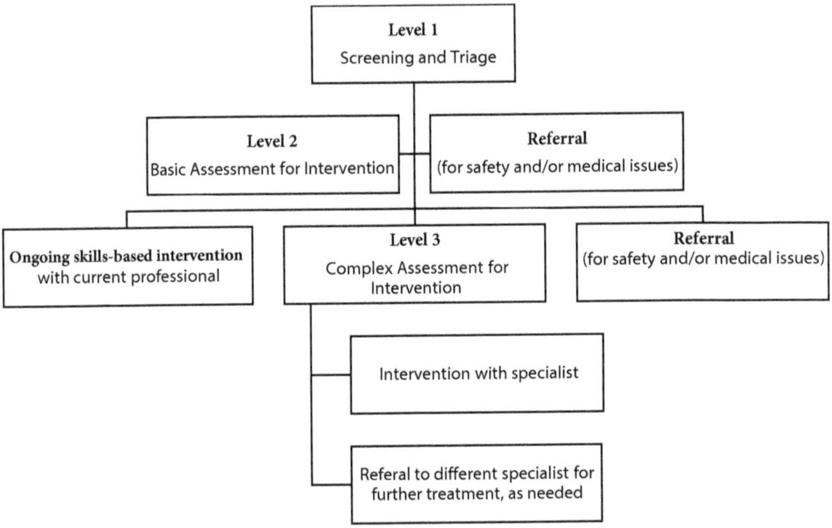

The model presented here describes three levels of assessment (Heath & Nixon, 2009, p. 143): "...first, the *triage* to determine the risk level of the youth; second, the *basic assessment for intervention* for use in referral or creation of skill-based intervention; and third, the *comprehensive assessment* for purposes of an intensive intervention". A hierarchical stepwise approach may function more efficiently and effectively than a unitary comprehensive assessment. A great potential in the complex approach to treatment can also be found in multisystemic therapy, concentrating on all the main systems with which an adolescent interacts (McDougal, Armstrong & Trainor, 2010). This approach focuses on effective parental skills and the support of the environment (school, peers and other communities), whose integrated part is also the support of pro-social activities[108] (Wood et al. 2001; Trainor & Wood, 2001; Huey et al., 2004; Ougrin et al., 2012).

6.3 The Specifics of Hospital Care for Self-Harming Adolescents

The possibility of hospitalisation of self-harming individuals is indicated especially in such acts of self-harm which are related to rather serious injuries, if psychopathology occurs, and possibly in cases of signs of suicidal behaviour.

Adolescent individuals are most often hospitalised after an act of self-harm by poisoning, but a higher risk of repeated self-harm is for example in case of cutting (Storey et al., 2005; Lilley, Owens & Horrocsk, 2008). Ougrin et al. (2012) in his overview study describe a standard procedure used in the USA for self-harming adolescents younger than 16 years: if self-harming behaviour is discovered, such an individual should be immediately accepted in a medical ward for children and assessed by a professional specialising in children and adolescents,[109] and, in cooperation with the patient and his/her caregiver, a plan for outpatient treatment must be agreed on before he/she is released from hospital care. A crisis plan should also be designed – prevention of a suicidal attempt. Butler & Longhitano (2008), in this context, draw attention to the necessity of the participation and cooperation of a multifield team of specialists and a follow-up treatment after completing hospitalisation.[110] On the other hand, Poustie & Nevill (2004, p. 35) highlight the necessity of an individual and human approach to every self-harming person. According to these authors, self-harm should be perceived in the following manner: "Perhaps this condition should be regarded as an enduring long-term health problem and support services should be configured around people rather than diagnoses."

---

108 Multisystemic Therapy (MST) versus psychiatric hospitalisation was associated with a reduction of suicidal attempts in a sample of adolescents with a range of psychiatric emergencies (Ougrin et al., 2012).

109 Nevertheless, being accepted to a ward can paradoxically strengthen self-harming tendencies in some patients.

110 Vaiva et al. (2006) state that telephone contact with an experienced psychiatrist 1 to 3 months after hospitalisation can lower the number of subsequent episodes of self-harm.

In adolescents who, apart from self-harm, show some other serious clinical symptoms, for example affective disorders, therapeutic approaches focused primarily on depressive symptoms prove useful – in this case, pharmacological treatment by antidepressants and mood stabilizers is in order, for instance a cognitive behavioural one. In these cases, adolescents are most often medicated with Fluoxetine, or Citalopram or Sertraline – each psychiatric medication needs to be carefully considered, especially its possible negative side effects. Psychopharmacology should focus on treating underlying psychiatric disorders. No medications are specifically effective for treating suicidal thoughts, suicidal behaviours, or self-harm because some evidence suggests that antidepressants may trigger suicidal thoughts in a small proportion of youth, but the benefits of antidepressants outweigh the risk of suicidal thoughts (Peterson, Feedenthal & Coles., 2010). Precautions should be taken when prescribing medication for self-harming adolescents (Jick, Kaye & Jick, 2004). For example, benzodiazepines may cause disinhibition, and larger quantities of medication could be lethal in an overdose (Bridge et al., 2007). Simon (2006), in this context, stresses: "If possible, arrange for parents or guardians to monitor medication use."

There remains considerable uncertainty concerning which forms of psychosocial and physical treatments of patients who harm themselves are most effective. On the basis of the carried out meta-analysis of the results of comparative studies on psychosocial intervention, Hawton et al. (1998) claim that the results of this systematic review indicate that currently there is insufficient evidence on which to make firm recommendations about the most effective forms of treatment for patients who have recently deliberately harmed themselves. Nevertheless, a great majority of self-harming adolescents never seek help of a psychologist, psychiatrist, doctor, or another adult person (Hrubá, Klimusová & Burešová, 2012; Hawton, Saunders & O'Connor, 2012).

Barriers to help-seeking include fear of negative reactions from others, including stigmatisation, fear of confidentiality being breached and fear of being seen as attention-seeking. Few facilitators of help-seeking were identified (Rowe et al., 2014). Of the very small part of adolescents who actively seek help when solving problems with their own self-harm, most of them turn to their peers, who are not ready to give such help and often do not even have the basic knowledge about the existing supporting systems of the available and adequate psychological, psychiatric, and possibly also medical care. Barriers to help-seeking (Favazza, 1999; Mazelis, 2008) and the lack of knowledge of where to seek help can, therefore, significantly complicate seeking help at the moment when the adolescent individual is motivated to take such a step in a difficult personal situation. Thus, the attention of specialists focusing on self-harm in adolescence should concentrate not only on searching for the most appropriate approaches to treating this highly risky type of behaviour, but also on systematic increasing of both professional and non-professional public awareness of the possibilities and ways of treatment, especially of the system of institutional support providing this type of care.

Summary

The publication examines the ever pressing issue of self-harm in adolescence in a complex way and concentrates on both historical context of the development of the classification system of self-harm and terminological anchoring of the bases for self-harm At the same time, it presents an overview of principal theoretical standpoints for self-harm as well as the models of self-harming behaviour which are based on them. In the context of the results of current research studies, it describes its prevalence, aetiology and comorbidity, and focuses on the specifics of this risky form of behaviour in the process of adolescence, including the impact of the developmental changes on its development. It presents in detail the basic protective and risky factors of self-harm and all the important influences which contribute to its final image. It offers a basic overview of diagnostic tools presently used in both research and clinical practice, and completes it with an outline of fundamental approaches to prevention, therapy and treatment of self-harm in adolescence.

Unlike other publications concentrating on this subject, the presented study includes the results of a unique research study, which was carried out with the help of the author. It maps the lexical trace of the term self-harm in adolescents and also the differences in the perception of this term between adolescents without any experience with self-harm, with a vicarious experience with self-harm, and with their own, often repeated, experience with this behaviour. These differences contribute to the complex picture of self-harm in this key and also risky developmental period.

List of Abbreviations

CASE	Child & Adolescent Self-harm in Europe Study
DSH	Deliberate Self Harm
DSHI	Deliberate Self-Harm Inventory
DSM-V™	Diagnostic and Statistical Manual of Mental Disorders – fifth edition
FASM	Functional Assessment of Self-Mutilation
ICD	International Classification of Diseases and Related Health Problems
ISAS	Inventory of Statements About Self-injury
ISHQ	Impulsive and Self-Harm Questionnaire
K-SADS-PL	Kiddie-Sads-Present and Lifetime Version
NSSI	Non Suicidal Self Injury
OCD	Obsessive Compulsive Disorder
OSI	Ottawa Self-Injury Inventory
SHBQ	Self-harm Behavior Questionnaire
SHI	Self-harm Inventory
SHQ	Self harm Questionnaire
SISRI	Self-Injury Self-Report Inventory
SITBI	Self-Injurious Thoughts and Behaviors Inventory
SIQ	Self-Injury Questionnaire
SM	Self-Mutilation
SOSI	The Signs of Self-Injury Program
RSM	Repetitive Self-Mutilation Syndrome

References

Achenbach, T. (1991). *Manual for the Child Behavior Checklist/4 – 18 and 1991 Profile*. Burlington, VT: University of Vermont Department of Psychiatry.

American Psychological Association (2013). *Diagnostic and statistical manual of mental disorders* (5th ed.). Washington, DC: APA.

Asarnow, J. R., Baraff, L., Berk, M., Grob, C., Devich-Navarro, M., Suddath, R., Piacentini, J., Rotheram-Borus, M. J., Cohen, D., & Tang, L. (2011). Effects of an emergency department mental health intervention for linking pediatric suicidal patients to follow-up mental health treatment: A randomized controlled trial. *Psychiatric Services*, 62(11), 1303–1309.

Asarnow, J. R., Porta, G., Spirito, A., Emslie, G., Clarke, G., Wagner, K. D., Vitiello, B., Keller, M., Birmaher, B., McCracken, J., Mayers, T., Berk, M., & Brent, D. A. (2011). Suicide attempts and nonsuicidal self-injury in the treatment of resistant depression in adolescents: Findings from the TORDIA Study. *Journal of the American Academy of Child and Adolescent Psychiatry*, 50(8), 772–781.

Baetens, I., Claes, L., Hasking, P., Smits, D., Grietens, H., Onghena, P., & Martin, G. (2015). The relationship between parental expressed emotions and NSSI: The mediating roles of self-criticism and depression. *Journal of Child and Family Studies*, 24, 491–498.

Bertolote, J. M. & Fleischmann, A. (2002). Suicide and psychiatric diagnosis: a worldwide perspective. *World Psychiatry*, 1, 181–85.

Berzonsky, M. D. (1989). Identity style: Conceptualization and measurement. *Journal of Adolescent research*, 4, 268–282.

Berzonsky, M. D. (2008). Identity formation: The role of identity processing style and cognitive processes. *Personality and Individual Differences*, 44, 645–655.

Blatný, M. (2010). *Psychologie osobnosti: hlavní témata, současné přístupy* [Psychology of personality: Main topics, contemporary approaches]. Praha: Grada.

Brausch, A. M. & Gutierrez, P. M. (2009). The Role of Body Image and Disordered Eating as Risk Factors for Depression and Suicidal Ideation in Adolescents. *Suicide Life Threat behavior*, 39(1), 58–71.

Brausch, A. M. & Gutierrez, P. M. (2010). Differences in Non-Suicidal Self-Injury and Suicide Attempts in Adolescents. *Journal of Youth Adolescence*, 39, 233–242.

Bridge, J. A., Iyengar, S., & Salary, C. B. (2007). Clinical response and risk for reported suicidal ideation and suicide attempts in pediatric antidepressant treatment: a meta-analysis of randomized controlled trials. *Journal of the American Medical Association*, 297(15), 1683–1696.

Brown, S. A. (2009). Personality and non-suicidal deliberate self-harm: Trait differences among a non-clinical population. *Psychiatry Research*, 169, 28–32.

Brown, M. Z., Comtois, K. A., & Linehan, M. M. (2002). Reasons for suicide attempts and nonsuicidal self-injury in women with borderline personality disorder. *Journal of Abnormal Psychology*, 111, 198–202.

Brunner, R., Parzer, P., Haffner, J., Steen, R., Roos, J., Klett, M., & Resch, F. (2007). Prevalence and psychological correlates of occasional and repetitive deliberate self-harm in adolescents. *Archives of pediatrics & adolescent medicine*, 161(7), 641–649.

Burešová, I. & Hrubá, V. (2012). Výskyt sebepoškozujícího jednání mezi dětmi školního věku. Pilotní studie [The prevalence of self-harm behaviour in school-age chidren. A pilot study]. In A. Heretik, E. Rošková (Eds.), *Zbornik Filozofickej fakulty Univerzity Komenskeho v Bratislave PSYCHOLOGICA XLI* (pp. 77–93). Bratislava: STIMUL, FiF UK.

Burešová, I. & Klimusová, H. (2014). Relationships with parents and peers, attitudes towards school, and preferred spare-time activities in young adolescents reporting self-harm. In C. Pracana (Ed.), *Advances in Psychology and Psychological Trends Series - Psychology Applications & Developments* (pp. 45–54). Lisboa, Portugal: InScience Press.

Burešová, I., Bartošová, K., & Čerňák, M. (2015). Connection between parenting styles and self-harm in adolescence. In Z. Bekirogullari and M. Yagmur Minas (Eds.), *Procedia Social and Behavioral Sciences, 171* (pp. 1106–1113). Amsterdam: ELSEVIER.

Burešová, I., Vrbová, M., & Čerňák, M. (2015). Personality characteristic of adolescent self-harmers. In Z. Bekirogullari and M. Yagmur Minas (Eds.), *Procedia Social and Behavioral Sciences, 171* (pp. 1118–1127). Amsterdam: ELSEVIER.

Butler, J. & Longhitano, C. (2008). Self-harm. *Medicine*, 36(9), 455–458.

Butler, J. (2012). Self-harm. *Medicine*, 40 (12), 650–653.

Byrnes, J., P. (2008). Piaget's cognitive- developmental theory. In M. H. Haith, & J. B. Benson. (2008). *Encyclopedia of infant and early childhood development*. San Diego: Academic press, 543–552.

Bywaters, P. & Rolfe, A. (2002). *Look Beyond the Scars: Understanding and Respon-ding to self-injury and self-harm*. London: NCH.

Carli, V., Jovanovic, N., Podlešek, A., Rihmer, Z., Maggi, S., Marusic, D., Cesaro, C., Marusic, A., & Sarchiapone, M. (2010). The role of impulsivity in self-mutilators, suicide ideators and suicide attempters — A study of 1265 male incarcerated individuals. *Journal of Affective Disorders*, 123, 116–122.

Carlstedt, R. H. (2010). *Handbook of Integrative Clinical Psychology, Psychiatry, and Behavioral Medicine: Perspectives, Practices, and Research*. New York: Springer Publishing Company.

Caspi, A., Sugden, K., Moffitt, T. E., Taylor, A., Craig, I. W., Harrington, H., McClay, J., Mill, J., Martin, J., Braithwaite, A., & Poulton. (2003). Influence of life stress on depression: Moderation by a polymorphism in the 5-HTT gene. *Science*, 301(5631), 386–389.

Cerutti, R., Manca, M., Presaghi, F., & Gratz, K. L. (2011). Prevalence and correlates of deliberate self-harm among a community sample of Italian adolescents. *Journal of Adolescence*, 34, 337–347.

Ciuhodaru, T., Iorga, M., & Romedea, S. N. (2012). Risk factors for non-lethal self-harm by substance abuse. *Procedia Social and Behavioral Sciences*, 33, 761–765.

Claes, L., Houben, A., Vandereycken, W., Bijttebier, P., & Muehlenkamp, J. (2010). Brief report: The Association between non-suicidal self-injury, self-concept and acquaintance with elf-injurious peers in a sample of adolescents. *Journal of adolescence*, 33, 775–778.

Claes, L. & Muehlenkamp, J. J. (2014). *Non-Suicidal Self-Injury in Eating Disorders: Advancements in Etiology*. Berlin: Springer Science & Business Media.

Claes, L. & Vandereycken, W. (2007). Self-injurious behavior: Differential diagnosis and functional differentiation. *Comprehensive Psychiatry*, 48, 137–144.

Claes, L. & Vandereycken, W. (2007). The Self-Injury Questionnaire-Treatment Related (SIQ-TR): Construction, reliability, and validity in a sample of female eating disorder patients. In P. M. Goldfarb (Eds.), *Psychological Tests and Testing Research Trends* (pp. 111–139). New York: Nova Science Publishers.

Claes, L., Houben, A., Vandereycken, W., Bijttebier, P., & Muehlenkamp, J. (2012). Brief report: The association between non-suicidal self-injury, self-concept and acquaintance with self-injurious peers in a sample of adolescents. *Journal of Adolescence*, 33(5), 775–778.

Cloutier, P. F. & Humphreys, L. (2009). Measurement of self-injury in adolescents. In M. K. Nixon, N. L. Heath (Eds.), *Self-injury in youth: The essential guide to assessment and intervention* (pp. 115–142). New York: Routledge Press.

Cloutier, P. & Nixon, K. M. (2005). Ottawa Self-Injury Inventory. Available from http://www.insync-group.ca/publications/OSI-2015-English-v3.1.pdf [Accessed 29 February 2016].

Collins, W. A. & Steinberg, L. (2006). Adolescent development in interpersonal context. In W. Damon & N. Eisenberg (Eds.), *Handbook of child Psychology*: Social, emotional and personality development (pp. 1003–1067). NY: Wiley.

Conterio, K., Lader, W., & Bloom, J., K. (1998). *Bodily Harm: The Breakthrough Healing Program for Self-Injurers*. New York: Hyperion.

Cooper, J., Kapur, N., Webb, R., Lawlor, M., Guthrie, E., Mackway-Jones, K., & Appleby, L. (2005). Suicide After Deliberate Self-Harm: A 4-Year Cohort Study. *The American Journal of Psychiatry*, 162(2), 297–303.

Cooper, J., Kapur, N., Dunning, J., Guthrie, E., Appleby, L., & Mackaway-Jones, K. (2006). A Clinical Tool for Assessing Risk After Self-Harm. *Annals of Emergency Medicine*, 48(4), 459–467.

Coughlan, H., Tiedt, L., Clarke, M., Kelleher, I., Tabish, J., Molloy, C., Harley, M., & Cannon, M. (2014). Prevalence of DSM-IV mental disorders, deliberate self-harm and suicidal ideation in early adolescence: An Irish population-based study. *Journal of Adolescence*, 37, 1–9.

Crawford, T., Geraghty, W., Street, K., & Simonoff, E. (2003). Staff knowledge and attitudes towards deliberate self-harm in adolescents. *Journal of Adolescence*, 26(5), 623–633.

Cumella, E. J., Eberly, M. C., & Wall, A. D. (2008). *Eating disorders. A handbook of Christian treatment*. Nashville: Remuda Ranch.

Cyr, M., McDuff, P., Wright, J., Thériault, C., & Cinq-Mars, C. (2005). Clinical correlates and repetition of self-harming behaviors among adolescent victims of sexual abuse. *Journal of Child Sexual Abuse*, 14(2), 49–68.

Čech, R., Popescu, I., & Altmann, G. (2014). *Metody kvantitativní analýzy (nejen) básnických textů* [The methods of quantitative analysis (not only) poetical texts]. Olomouc: Univerzita Palackého.

Dakanalis, A., Madeddu, F., Clerici, M., Riva, G., & Zanetti, M. A. (2013). The role of body shame and body image avoidant behaviours in deliberate self-harm. *Journal of Psychosomatic Research*, 74(6), 543–560.

Darche, M. A. (1990). Psychological factors differentiating self-mutilating and non-self-mutilating adolescent inpatient females. *The Psychiatric Hospital*, 21, 31–35.

De Leo, D & Heller, T. S. (2004). Who are the kids who self-harm? An Australian self-report school survey. *Medical Journal of Australia*, 181(3), 140–144.

Dervic, K., Oquendo, M. A., Grunebaum, M. F., Ellis, S., Burke, A. K., & Mann, J. J. (2004). Religious affiliation and suicide attempt. *American Journal of Psychiatry*, 161, 2303–08.

American Psychiatric Association. (2013). *Diagnostic and statistical manual of mental disorders: DSM-VTM*. Fifth edition. Washington, DC: American Psychiatric Association.

Di Clemente, R. J., Ponton, L. E., & Hartley, D. (1991). Prevalence and correlates of cutting behavior: Risk for HIV transmission. *Journal of the American Academy of Child and Adolescent Psychiatry*, 30, 735–739.

DiClemente, R. J., Santelli, J. S., & Crosby, R. A. (2009). *Adolescent health: Understanding and preventing risk behaviors*. San Francisco, CA: John Wiley & Sons.

Di Pierro, R., Sarno, I., Perego, S., Gallucci, M., & Madeddu, F. (2012). Adolescent nonsuicidal self-injury: The effects of personality traits, family relationships and maltreatment on the presence and severity of behaviours. *European Child & Adolescent Psychiatry*, 21(9), 511–20.

Doctors, S. (1981). The symptom of delicate self-cutting in adolescent females: A developmental view. In S. C. Feinstein, J. G. Looney, A. Z. Schwartzberg, & A. D. Sorosky (Eds.), *Adolescent psychiatry*, 9, 443–460.

Dominique, E. & Roe-Sepowitz. (2005). *Indicators of Self-Mutilation: Youth in Custody*. The Florida State University College of Social Work.

Duffy, D. F. (2006). Self-injury. *Psychiatry*, 5(8): 263–5.

Dugas, E., Low., N. C., Rodriguez, D., Burrows, S., Contreras, G., Chaiton, M., & OĹoughlin, J (2012). Early predictors of suicidal ideation in young adults. *Canadian Journal of Psychiatry. Revue Cannadienne de Psychiatre*, 57(7), 429–436.

Dyl, J. (2008). Understanding cutting in adolescents: Prevalence, prevention and intervention. *The Brown University Child and Adolescent Behavior Letter*, 24(3), 4–6.

Emerson, L. E. (1913). The Case of Miss A: A Preliminary Report of a Psychoanalytic Study and Treatment. *Psychoanalitical. Review*, 1, 41–54.

Evans. E., Hawton, K., & Rodham, K. (2004). Factors associated with suicidal pheno-mena in adolescents: a systematic review of populationbased studies. *Clinical Psychology Review*, 24, 957–79.

Evren, C. & Evren, B. (2005). Self-mutilation in substance-dependent patients and relationship with childhood abuse and neglect, alexithymia and temperament and character dimensions of personality. *Drug and Alcohol Dependence*, 80, 15–22.

Favazza, A. R. (1987). *Bodies under Siege. Self-mutilation in Culture and Psychiatry*. London: John Hopkins University Press.

Favazza, A. R. & Conterio, K. (1988). The plight of chronic self-mutilators. *Community Mental Health Journal*, 24, 22–30.

Favazza, A. R. & Conterio, K. (1989). Female habitual self-mutilators. *Acta Psychiatrica Scandinavica*, 79, 282–289.

Favazza, A. R. & Rosenthal, R. J. (1990). Varieties of pathological self-mutilation. *Behavioral Neurology*, 3, 77–85.

Favazza, A. R. (1996). *Bodies under Siege. Bodies under Siege: Self-mutilation and Body Modification in Culture and Psychiatry*. Baltimore: John Hopkins University Press.

Favazza, A. R. (1998). The coming age of self-mutilation. *The Journal of Nervous and Mental Disease*, 186(5), 259–68.

Favazza, A. R. (1999). Self-mutilation. In D. G. Jacobs (Eds.), *The Harvard Medical School guide to suicide assessment and intervention* (pp. 125–145). San Francisco, CA; Jossey-Bass.

Favazza, A. R. (2011). Feral and isolated children. *British Journal of Medical Psychology*, 50(1), 105–111.

Fechner, P., Y. (2002). Gender differenes in puberty. *Journal of Adolescent Health*, 30, 44–48.

Feldman, D., H. (2004). Piaget's stages: the unfinished symphony of cognitive development. *New Ideas in Psychology*, 22, 175–231.

Fergusson, D., Woodward, L., & Horwood, L. (2000). Risk factors and life processess associated with the onset of suicidal behaviour during adolescence and early adulthood. *Psychological Medicine*, 30(1), 23–39.

Fletcher, A. C., Steinberg, L., & Williams-Wheeler, M. (2004). Parental influences on adolescent problem behavior. *Child Development*, 75(3), 781–796.

Friedman, M., Glasser, M., Laufer, E., Laufer, M., & Wohl, M. (1972). Attempted suicide and self-mutilation in adolescence: Some observations from a psychoanalytic research project. *British Journal of Psychoanalysis*, 53, 179–183.

Garcia, L. F., Aluja, A., & Barrio, V. D. (2006). Effects of personality, rearing styles and social values on adolescents' socialisation process. *Personality and Individual Differences*, 40, 1671–1682.

Glenn, C. R. & Klonsky, E. D. (2010). A multimethod analysis of impulsivity in non-suicidal self-injury. Personality Disorders: Theory, Research, and Treatment, 1, 67–75.

Glenn, V. S. E. & Klonsky, E. D. (2012). Is non-suicidal self-injury an "addiction"? A comparison of craving in substance use and non-suicidal selfinjury. *Psychiatry Research*, 197, 73–77.

González-Forteza, C., Alvarez-Ruiz, M., Saldaňa-Hernández, A., & Carreňo-García, S., et al. (2005). Prevalence of Deliberate Self-harm in Teenage Students in the State of Guanajuato, Mexico: 2003. *Social Behavior and Personality*, 33(8), 777–791.

Gordon, L. F., Abby, L. G., Paul, L. H., & Wekerle, C. (2012). Predictors of deliberate self-harm behavior among emerging adolescents: An initial test of a self-punitiveness model. *Current Psychology*, 31(1), 49–64.

Graff, H. & Mallin, R. (1967). The syndrome of the wrist cutter. *American Journal of Psychiatry*, 124, 74–80.

Gratz, L. K. (2001). Measurement of deliberate self-harm: Preliminary data on the deliberate self-harm inventory. *Journal of Psychopathology and Behavioral Assessment, 23*, 253–263.

Groschwitz, M. R. C., & Plener, P. L. (2012). The Neurobiology of non-suicidal Self-injury (NSSI): A review. *Suicidology Online*, 3, 24–32.

Gross, J. J. (1999). Emotion regulation: Past, present, and future.*Cognition and Emotion*, 13, 551–573.

Gunter, T. D., Chinball, J. T., Antoniak, S. K., Philibert, R. A., & Hollenbeck, N. (2011). Predictors of suicidal ideation, suicide attempts, and self-harm without lethal intent in a community corrections sample. *Journal of Criminal Justice,* 39, 238–245.

Gutierrez, P. M., Osman, A., Barrios, F. X., & Kopper, B. A. (2001). Development and initial validation of the Self-Harm Behavior Questionnaire. *Journal of Personality Assessment*, 77, 475–490.

Hallab, L. & Covic, T. (2010). Deliberate self-harm: The interplay between attachment and stress. *Behaviour Change*, 27(02), 93–103.

Hargus, E., Hawton, K., & Rodham, K. (2009). Distinguishing between subgroups of adolescents who self-harm. *Suicide & Life – Threatening Behavior*, 39(5), 518–37.

Harned, M. S., Najavits, L. M., Weiss, R. D. (2006). Self-Harm and Suicidal Behavior in Women with Comorbid PTSD and Substance Dependence. *American Journal on Addictions*, 15(5), 392–935.

Harrington, R. (2001). Depression, suicide and deliberate self-harm in adolescence. *British Medical Bulletin*, 57 (1), 47–60.

Hasking, P., Coric, S., Swannell, S., Martin, G., Thompson, K. H. & Frost, A. (2010). Brief report: Emotion regulation and coping as moderators in the relationship between personality and self-injury. *Journal of Adolescence*, 33(5), 767–773.

Haviger, J., Havigerová, J. M., & Loudová, I. (2014). *Lexikální stopa pojmu Rodina* [The lexical trace of the term Family]. Hradec Královė: Gaudeamus.

Hawkins, J. D., Herrenkohl, T. I., Farrington, D. P., Brewer, D., Catalano, R. F., & Harachi, T. W., et al. (2000). Predictors of youth violence. *OJJDP Juvenile Justice Bulletin*, 1–11.

Hawton, K., Kingsbury, S., Steinhardt, K., James, A., & Fagg, J. (1999). Repetition of deliberate self-harm by adolescents: the role of psychological factors. *Journal of Adolescence*, 22, 369–378.

Hawton, K., Rodham, K., Evans, E., & Weatherall, R. (2002). Deliberate self harm in adolescents: Self report survey in schools in England. *British Medical Journal*, 325, 1207–1211.

Hawton, K. & Rodham, K. (2006). *By Their Own Young Hand: Deliberate Self-harm and Suicidal Ideas in Adolescents*. London: Kingsley Publishers.

Hawton, K., Rodham, K., Evans, E., & Weatherall, R. (2002). Deliberate self harm in adolescents: self report survey in schools in England. *British Medical Journal*, 325, 1207–1211.

Hawton, K., Aresman, E., Townsend, E., Bremner, S., Feldman, E., Goldney, R., & Gunell, D., et al. (1998). Deliberate self harm: Systematic review of efficacy of psychosocial and pharmacological treatments in preventing repetition. *British Medical Journal*, 317(7156), 441–447.

Hawton, K. & Harris, L. (2007). Deliberate self-harm in young people: Characteristics and subsequent mortality in a 20-year cohort of patients presenting to hospital. *Journal of Clinical Psychiatry*, 68(10), 1574–1583.

Hawton, K., Harriss, L., & Rodham, K. (2010). How adolescents who cut themselves differ from those who take overdose. *Europian Child & Adolescent Psychiatry*, 19, 513–523.

Hawton, K., Saunders, E. A., & O'Connor, R. (2012). Self-harm and suicide in adolescents. *Lancet*, 379, 2373–82.

Hawton, K., Bergen, H., Waters, K., Ness, J., Cooper, J., Stegg, S. & Kapur, N. (2012). Epidemiology and nature of self-harm in children and adolescents: findings from the multicentre study of self-harm in England. *European Child & Adolescent Psychiatry*, 21(7), 369–377.

Hawton, K., Saunders, K., Topiwala, A. & Haw, C. (2013). Psychiatric disorders in patiens presenting to hospital following self-harm: A systemic review. *Journal of Affective Disorders*, 15(3), 821–830.

Hayward, CH. & Sanborn, K. (2002): Puberty and emergence of gender differences in psychopatology. *Journal of Adolescent Health*, 30, 49–58.

Healy, E., Saha, S., Subotsky, F., & Fombonne, E. (2002). Emergency presentations to an inner-city adolescent psychiatric service. *Journal of Adolescence*, 25(4), 397–404.

Heath, N. L., Toste, J. R., Nedecheva, T., & Charlebois, A. (2008). An examination of nonsuicidal self-injury among college students. *Journal of Mental Health Counseling*, 30(2), 137–156.

Heath, N. L., Nixon, M. K. (2009). Assessment of nonsuicidal self-injury in youth. In M. K. Nixon, N. L. Heath (Eds.), *Self-injury in youth: The essential guide to assessment and intervention* (pp. 143–170). New York: Routledge Press.

Herpetz, S. (1995). Self-injurious behavior: Psychopathological and nosological characteristics in subtypes of self-injurers. *Acta Psychiatrica Scandinavica*, 91, 57–68.

Hicks, K. M. & Hinck, S. M. (2008). Concept analysis of self-mutilation. *Journal of Advanced Nursing*, 64(4), 408–413.

Hill, P., L., Allemand, M., Grob-Zehnder, S., Peng, A., Morgenthaler, CH., & Kappler, CH. (2013). Longitudinal relations between personality traits and aspects of identity formation during adolescence. *Journal of Adolescence*, 36, 413–421.

Hilt, L. M., Nock, M. K., Lloyd-Richardson, E. E., & Prinstein, M. J. (2008). Longitudinal study of an interpersonal model of non-suicidal self-injury among young adolescents. *Journal of Early Adolescence*, 28, 455–469.

Himber, J. (1994). Blood rituals: Self-cutting in female psychiatric inpatients. *Psychotherapy*, 31, 620–631.

Holi, M., M., Pelkonen, M., & Karlsson, L., et al. (2005). Psychometric properties and clinical utility of the Scale for Suicidal Ideation (SSI) in adolescents. *BMC Psychiatry*, *5*(1), 8.

Honkalampi K., Koivumaa-Honkanen H., Antikainen R., Haatainen K., Hintikka J., & Viinama, H. (2004): Relationships Among Alexithymia, Adverse Childhood Experiences, Sociodemographic Variables, and Actual Mood Disorder: A 2-Year Clinical Follow-Up Study of Patients With Major Depressive Disorder. *Psychosomatics*, 45, 197–204.

Hrubá, V., Burešová, I., & Čerňák, M. (2015). Self-harming behavior and its relation with previous psychological or psychiatric care. *The European Journal of Social & Behavioural Sciences*, 13(2), 1865–1875.

Hrubá, V., Klimusová, H., & Burešová, I. (2012). Výskyt, formy a vybrané souvislosti sebepoškozování u dětí staršího školního věku [The prevalence, forms and selected correlations of self-harm in older school-age children]. In P. Halama, R. Hanák, R. Masaryk. *Sociálne procesy a osobnosť* (pp. 118–122). Bratislava: Ústav experimentálnej psychológie SAV.

Hsu, Y-F., Chen, P-F., & Lung, F-W. (2013). Parental bonding and personality characteristics of first episode intention to suicide or deliberate selfharm without a history of mental disorders. *BMC Public Health*, 13, 421.

Huan, J., S., Norman, G., J., Zabinski, M., F., Calfas, K., & Patrick, K. (2007). Body Image and Self-Esteem among Adolescents Undergoing an Intervention Targeting Dietary and Physical Activity Behaviors. *Journal of Adolescent Health*, 40, 245–251.

Huey, S. J., Henggeler, S. W., Rowland, M. D., Halliday-Boykins, C. A., Cunningham, P. B., Pickrel, S. G., & Edwards, J. (2004). Multisystemic Therapy Effects on Attempted Suicide by Youths Presenting Psychiatrich Emergencies. *Journal American Academy Child and Adolescent Psychiatry*, 43(2), 183–190.

Hulten, A., Jiang, G. X., Wasserman, D., Hawton, K., Hjelmeland, H., De Leo, D. et al. (2001). Repetition of attempted suicide among teenagers in Europe: frequency, timing and Risk factors. *European Child & Adolescent Psychiatry*, 10(3), 161–169.

Chapman, A. L., Gratz, K. L., & Brown, M. Z. (2006). Solving the puzzle of deliberate self-harm: The experiential avoidance model. *Behaviour Research and Therapy*, 44, 371–394.

Chowanec, G. D., Josephson, A. M., Coleman, C., & Davis, H. (1991).Self-harming Behavior in Incarcerated Male Delinquent Adolescents. *Journal of the American Academy of Child and Adolescent Psychiatry*, 30(2), 202–207.

In-Albon, T., Ruf, C., & Schmid, M. (2013a). Proposed diagnostic criteria for the DSM-5 of nonsuicidal self-injury in female adolescents: Diagnostic and clinical correlates. *Psychiatry Journal*, 2013, 1–12.

In-Albon, T., Bűrli, M., Ruf, C., & Schmid, M. (2013b). Non-suicidal self-injury and emotion regulation: A review on facial emotion recognition and facial mimicry. *Child and Adolescent Psychiatry and Mental Health*, 7(5), 1–11.

Izutsu, T., Shimotsu, S., Matsumoto, T., Okada, T., Kikuchi, A., Kojimoto, M., et al. (2006). Deliberate Self-harm and Childhood Hyperactivity in Junior High School Students. *European Child & Adolescent Psychiatry,* 15(3), 172–176.

Jacobson C. M. & Gould, M. (2007). The epidemiology and phenomenology of non-suicidal self-injurious behavior among adolescents: a critical review of the literature. *Archives of Suicide Research, 11*, 129–147.

Jacobson, C. M., Muehlenkamp, J. J., Millerc, A. L., & Turner, J. B. (2008). Psychiatric Impairment Among Adolescents Engaging in Different Types of Deliberate Self-Harm. *Journal of Clinical Child & Adolescent Psychology,* 37(2), 363–375.

Janis, I. B. & Nock, K. M. (2008). Behavioral Forecasts Do Not Improve the Prediction of Future Behavior: A Prospective Study of Self-Injury. *Journal of Clinical Psychology*, 64(10), 1164–1174.

Javdani, S., Sadeh, N., & Verona, E. (2011): Expanding our lens: Female pathways to antisocial behavior in adolescence and adulthood. *Clinical Psychology Review*, 31, 1324–1348.

Jick, H., Kaye J. A., & Jick S. S. (2004). Antidepressants and the risk of suicidal behaviors. *Journal of the American Medical Association*, 292, 338–343.

Juzwin, K. R. (2004). An Assessment Tool for Self-Injury: The Self-Injury Self-Report Inventory (SISRI). In J. L. Levitt, R. A. Sansone, L. Cohn (Eds.),

Self-Harm Behavior and Eating Disorders: Dynamics, Assessment, and Treatment (pp. 105–119). New York: Brunner-Rutledge.

Karukivi M., Hautala L., Kaleva O., Haapasalo-Pesu K., Liuksila P., Joukamaa M., & Saarijärvi, S. (2010): Alexithymia Is Associated With Anxiety Among Adolescents. *Journal of Affective Disorders*, 125, 383–387.

Kench, S. & Irwin, H., J. (2000). Alexithymia and childhood family environment. *Journal of Clinical Psychology*, 56, 737–745.

Kenny, R., Dooley, B., & Fitzgerald, A. (2013). Interpersonal relationships and emotional distress in adolescence. *Journal of Adolescence*, 36, 351–360.

Kesserling, T & Muller, U (2011). The concept of egocentrism in the context of Piaget's theory. *New Ideas in Psychology*, 29, 327–345.

Klimusová, H., Burešová, I., & Bartošová, K. (2013). The impact of parent-child and peer relationships on depressive symptoms and self-esteem in early adolescence. In C. Pracana, L. Silva (Eds.), *International Psychological Applications Conference and Trends. Book of Proceedings* (pp. 26–30). Lisbon: Wiars.

Klonsky, E., D. (2007). The functions of deliberate self-injury: A review of the evidence. *Clinical Psychology Review*, 27(2), 226–239.

Klonsky, E. D. (2009). The functions of self-injury in young adults who cut themselves: Clarifying the evidence for affect-regulation. *Psychiatry Research*, 166, 260–268.

Klonsky, E. D., Glenn, C. R. (2009). Assessing the functions of non-suicidal self-injury: Psychometric properties of the Inventory of Statements About Self-injury (ISAS). *Journal of Psychopathology and Behavioral Assessment*, 31, 215–219.

Klonsky, E. D., Muehlenkamp, J., Lewis, S. P., & Walsh, B. (2011). *Nonsuicidal Self-Injury. Advances in Psychoteraphy. Evidence-Based Practise.* Hoegrefe Publishing.

Klonsky, E. D., Oltmanns, T. F., & Turkheimer, E. (2003). Deliberate self-harm in a non-clinical population: Prevalence and psychological correlates. *American Journal of Psychiatry* 160, 1501–1508.

Klump, K. (2013). Puberty as a critical risk period for eating disorders: A review of human and animal studies. *Hormones and Behaviour*, 64, 399–410.

Koepke, S. & Denissen, J. J. A. (2012). Dynamics of identity development and separation- individuation in parent-child relationships during adolescence and emerging adulthood. A conceptual integration. *Developmental Review*, 32, 67–88.

Koutek, J. & Kocourková, J. (2003). *Sebevražedné chování: Současné poznatky o suicidalitě a její specifika u dětí a dospívajících* [Suicidal behaviour: Current knowledge about suicidality and its specifics in children and youths]. Praha: Portál.

Kreitman, N. (1977). *Parasuicide.* London: Wiley.

Krettenauer, T., Colasante, T., Buchmann, & M., Malti, T. (2013). The development of moral emotions and decision-making from adolescence to early adulthood: a 6-year longitudinal study. *Journal of Youth Adolescence*, 43(4), 583–96.

Kroger, J., Martinussen, M., & Marccia, J. E. (2010). Identity status change during adolescence and young adulthood: A meta- analysis. *Journal of Adolescence*, 33, 683–698.

Kvernmo, S. & Rosenvinge, J. H. (2009). Self-mutilation and suicidal behaviour in Sami and Norwegian adolescents: prevalence and correlates. *International Journal of Circumpolar Health*, 68(3), 235–248.

Langmeier, J. & Krejčířová, M. (2006). *Vývojová psychologie* [Developmental psychology]. Praha: Grada Publishing.

Latimer, S., Meade, T., & Tennat, A. (2013). Measuring engagement in deliberate self-harm behaviours: psychometric evaluation of six scales. *BMC Psychiatry*, 1–11.

Laukkanen, E., Rissanen, M. L., Honkalampi, K., Kylma, J., Tolmunen, T., & Hintikka, J. (2009). The Prevalence of self-cutting and other self-harm among 13- to 18-year-old Finnish adolescents. *Social Psychiatry and Psychiatric Epidemiology*, 44(1), 23–28.

Laye-Gindhu, A. & Schonert-Reichl, K. A. (2005). Nonsuicidal self-harm among community adolescents: Understanding the "whats" and "whys" of self-harm. *Journal of Youth and Adolescence*, 34(5), 447–457.

Leibenluft, E., Gardner, D. L., & Cowdry, R. W. (1987). The inner experience of the borderline self-mutilator. *Journal of Personality Disorders*, 1317–1324.

Lescano, C. M., Hadley, W. S., Beausoleil, N. I., Brown, L. K., D'eramo, D. & Zimskind, A. (2007). *Child Psychiatry Human Development*, 37(4), 325–336.

Levenkron, S. (1998). *Cutting: Understanding and Overcoming Self-Mutilation.* New York: W. W. Norton.

Levenkron, S. (2006). *Cutting: Understanding and Overcoming Self-Mutilation.* New York/London: W. W. Norton and Company.

Levitt, J. L., Sansone, R. A., & Cohn, L. (Eds.) (2004). *Self- Harm Behavior and Eating Disorders: Dynamics, Assessment and Treatment.* New York, Hove: Brunner-Routledge.

Lewis, L. M. (2007). No-harm contracts: a review of what we know. *Suicide Life Threat Behav*, 37, 50–57.

Lieberman, R. (2004). Understanding and Responding to Students Who Self-Mutilate. *Principal Leadership Magazine*, 4(7), 100.

Lilley, R., Owens, D., & Horrocsk, J. (2008). Hospital care and repetition following self-harm: a multicentre comparison of self-poisoning and self-injury. *British Journal of Psychiatry*, 192, 440–45.

Lilley, R. & Owens, D. (2009). Services for assessment, aftercare, and psychological treatment following selfharm. *Psychiatry*, 8(7), 246–252.

Lipschitz, D. S., Winegar, R. K., Nicolaou, A. L., Hartnick, E., Wolfson, M., & Southwick, S. M. (1999). Perceived abuse and neglect as risk factors for suicidal behaviour in adolescent inpatiens. *Journal of nervous and Mental Disease*, 187(1), 32–39.

Lloyd-Richardson, E. E., Perrine, N., Derker, L., & Kelley, M. L. (2007). Characteristics and functions of non-suicidal self-injury in a community sample of adolescents. *Psychological Medicine*, 37(08), 1183–1192.

Lumley M. A., Neely L. C., & Burger A. J. (2010). The Assessment of Alexithymia in Medical Settings: Implications for Understanding and Treating Health Problems. *Journal of Personality Assessement,* 89(3), 230–246.

Lundh, L. G., Karim, J., & Quilisch, E. (2007). Deliberate self-harm in 15-year-old adolescents: A pilot study with a modified version of the deliberate self-harm inventory. *Scandinavien Journal of Psychology*, 48, 33–41.

Macek, P. (2003). *Adolescence: psychologické a sociální charakteristiky dospívajících* [Adolescence: Psychological and social characteristics of adolescents]. Praha: Portál.

Madge, N., Hewitt, A., Hawton, K., De Wilde, E. J., Corcordan, P., Fekete, S. et al. (2008). Deliberate self-harm within an international community sample of young people: komparative findings from the Child & Adolescent Self-harm in Europe (CASE) Study. *The Journal of Child Psychology and Psychiatry*, 49, 667–677.

Madge, N., Hawton, K., McMahon, E. M., Corcoran, P., De Leo, D., De Wilde, E. J., & et al. (2011). Psychological characteristics, stressful life events and deliberate self-harm: findings from the Child & Adolescent Self-harm in Europe (CASE) Study. *European Child & Adolescent Psychiatry*, 20, 499–508.

Malone, K. M., Oquendo, M. A., Haas, G. L., Ellis, S. P., Li, S., Mann, J. J. (2000). Protective factors against suicidal acts in major depression: reasons for living. *American Journal of Psychiatry*, 157, 1084–88.

Mangall, J. & Yurkovich, E. (2008). A Literature Review of Deliberate Self-Harm. *Perspectives in Psychiatric Care*, 44(3), 175.

Martin, J., Cloutier, P. F., Levesque, C., Bureau, J. F., Lafontaine, M. F., & Nixon, M. K. (2013). Psychometric properties of the functions and addictive features scales of the Ottawa self-injury inventory: a preliminary investigation using a university sample. *Psychological Assessment, 25*(3), 1013–1018.

Matsunaga, H., Kiriike, N., Iwasaki, Y., Miyata, A., Matsui, T., Hagata, T., Yamagami, S., & Kaye, W., H. (2000). Multi-impulsivity among bulimic patients in Japan. *International Journal of Eating Disorders*, 27(3), 348–352.

Mazelis, R. (2008). *Living with and healing from self-injury (self-inflicted violence).* Brooklandville: Sidran Press.

McConnell, L. & Lewis, M. S. (2007). No-harm Contracts: A Review of What We Know. *Suicide and Life-Threatening Behavior*, 37(1), 50–87.

McDougal, T., Armstrong, M., & Trainor, G. (2010). *Hepling Children and Young People who Self-harm. An introduction to self-harming and suicidal behaviours for health professionals*. London: Routledge.

McLaughlin, J. A., Miller, P., & Warwick, H. (1996). Deliberate self-harm in adolescents: hopelessness, depression, problems and problem-solving. *Journal of Adolescence*, 19, 523–532.

McMahon, E. M., Reulbach, U., Keeley, H., Perry, I. J., & Arensman, E. (2010). Bullying victimisation, self harm and associated factors in Irish adolescent boys. *Social Science & Medicine*, 71, 1300–1307.

McMahon, M. E., Corcoran, P., McAulife, C., Keeley, H., Perry, I. J., & Arensman, E. (2013). Mediating effects of coping style on associations between mental healt factors and self-harm among adolescents. *Crisis*, 34(4), 242–250.

Meganck, R., Vanheule, S., Inslegers, R., & Dessmet, M. (2009): Alexithymia and Interpersonal Problems: A Study of Natural Language Use. *Personality and Individual Differences*, 47(8), 990–995.

Meltzer, H., Harrington, R., Goodman, R., & Jenkins, R. (2001). Children and adolescents who try to harm, hurt or kill themselves. London: Office for National Statistics.

Menninger, K. (1935). A psychoanalytic study of the significance of self-mutilation. *Psychoanalytic Quarterly*, 408–466.

Menninger, K. (1938). *Man against himself.* New York: Harcourt, Brace & World.

Messer, J. M. & Fremouw, W. J. (2008). A critical review of explanatory models for self-mutilating behaviors in adolescents. *Clinical Psychology Review*, 28, 162–178.

Mezinárodní klasifikace nemocí a přidružených zdravotních problémů [International classification of diseases and related health problems] (2008). MKN-10: Praha: Bomton Agency.

Miller, D. (1994). *Women who hurt themselves: A book of hope and understanding.* New York: Basic Books.

Miller, A. L., Rathus, J. H., & Linehan, M. M. (2007). *Dialectical behavior therapy with suicidal adolescents.* New York: The Guilford Press.

Miller, D. N. & Brock, S. E. (2010). *Identifying, Assessing, and Treating Self-Injury at schol.* New York: Springer Science & Business Media.

Mitchell, K. J. & Ybarra, M. L. (2007). Online behavior of youth who engage in self-harm provides clues for preventive intervention. *Preventive Medicine*, 45, 392–396.

Moran, P., Coffey, C., Romaniuk, H., Olsson, C., & Borschmann, R. (2012). *The natural history of self-harm from adolescence to young adulthood: a population-based cohort study.* The Lancet, 379 (9812), 236–243.

Motz, A. (2001). *The Psychology of Female Violence: Crimes Against the Body.* Hove: Routledge.

Mrug, S., Hoza, B., & Bukowski, W. M. (2008). Choosing or Being Chosen by Aggressive Disruptive Peers: Do They Contribute to Children's Externalizing and Internalizing Problems? *Journal of Abnormal Child Psychology*, 32(1), 53–65.

Muehlenkamp, J. J. & Gutierrez, P. M. (2004). An investigation of differences between elf-injurious behavior and suicide attemps in a sample of adolescents. *Suicide and Life Threatening Behavior*, 34(1), 12–23.

Muehlenkamp, J. J., Walsh, B. W., & McDade, M. (2010). Preventint non-suicidal selfinjury in adolescents: The sign sof self-injury program. *Journal of Youth and Adolescence*, 39(3), 306–313.

Muehlenkamp, J. J. & Brausch, A. M. (2012). Body image as a mediator of non-suicidal self-injury in adolescents. *Journal of Adolescence*, 35, 1–9.

Muehlenkamp, J. J., Claes, L., Havertape, L., & Plener, P. L. (2012). International prevalence of adolescent non-suicidal self-injury and deliberate self-harm. *Child and Adolescent Psychiatry and Mental Health*, 6:10.

Murray, K., Rieger, E., & Byrne, D. (2013). A longitudinal investigation of the mediating role of self-esteem and body importance in the relationship between stress and body dissatisfaction in adolescent females and males. *Body Image*, 10, 544–551.

Mustanski, B. & Liu, R. (2013). A longitudinal study of predictors of suicide attempts among lesbian, gay, bisexual, and transgender youth. *Archives of Sexual Behavior*, 42(3), 437–448.

Nichols, P. (2000). Bad body fever and deliberate self-injury. *Reclaiming Children and Youth*, 9(3), 151–156.

Nixon, M. K., Cloutier, P. F., & Aggarwal, S. (2002). Affect regulations and addictive aspects of repetitive self-injury in hospitalized adolescents. *Journal of the American Academy of Child and Adolescent Psychiatry*, 41(11), 1333–1341.

Nixon, M. K., Cloutier, P. F., & Jansson, S. M. (2008). Nonsuicidal self-harm in youth: A population-based survey. *Canadian Medical Association Journal*, 178(3), 306–312.

Nixon, M. K., Levesque, C., Preyde, M., Vanderkooy, J., & Cloutier, P. F. (2015). The Ottawa Self-Injury Inventory: Evaluation of an assessment measure of non-suicidal self-injury in an inpatient sample of adolescents. *Child and Adolescent Psychiatry and Mental Health*, 9, 26.

Nock, M. K. (2009). *Understanding Nonsuicidal Self-Injury: Origins, Assessment, and Treatment.* Washington: American Psychological Association.

Nock, M. K. (2012). Future Direction for the study of suicide and self-injury. *Journal of Clinical Child & Adolescent Psychology*, 41(2), 255–259.

Nock, M. K. & Prinstein, M. J. (2004). A Functional approach to the assessment of self-mutilative behavior. *Journal of Consulting and Clinical Psychology*, 72, 885–890.

Nock, M. K., Holmberg, E. B., Photos, V. I., & Michel, B. D. (2007). Self-injurious thoughts and behaviors interview: Development, reliability, and validity in an adolescent sample. *Psychological Assessment*, 19, 309–317.

Nock, M. K., Wedig, M. M., Janis, I. B., & Deliberto, T. L. (2008). *Self-Injurious Thoughts and Behaviors.* In J. Hunsley, E. J. Mash (Eds.), *A Guide to Assessments That Work* (pp. 158–177). New York: Oxford University Press.

Oerter, R. & Montada, L. (2002). *Entwicklungspsychologie.* Weinheim: Beltz.

Osuch, E. A., Payne, G. W. (2009). Neurobiological perspectives on self-injury. In M. K. Nixon, N. L. Heath (Eds.), *Self-injury in youth: The essential guide to assessment and intervention* (pp. 79–110). New York: Routledge Press.

Ougrin, D. & Boege, I. (2013). Brief report: The self harm questionnaire: A new tool designed to improve identification of self harm in adolescents. *Journal of Adolescence*, 36(1), 221–225.

Ougrin, D., Tranah, T., Leigh, E., Taylor, L., & Asarnow, J. R. (2012). Practitioner Review: Self-harm in adolescents. *The Journal of Child Psychology and Psychiatry*, 53(4), 337–350.

Ougrin, D., Tranah, T., Stahl, D., Moran, P., & Asarnow, J. R. (2015). Therapeutic Interventions for Suicide Attempts and Self-Harm in Adolescents: Systematic Review and Meta-Analysis. *Journal of the American Academy of Child and Adolescent Psychiatry*, 54(2), 97–107.

Ougrin, D. & Zundel, T. (2009). *Defining self-harm.* In D. Ourgin, T. Zundel (Eds.), *Self-Harm in Young People: A Therapeutic Assessment* manual (pp. 1–17). London: Hooder Arnold.

Paivio, S. C. & McCulloch, C. R. (2004). Alexithymia as a mediator between childhood trauma and self-injurious behaviors. *Child Abuse & Neglect*, 28, 339–354.

Pao, P. N. (1969). The syndrome of delicate self-cutting. *British Journal of Medical Psychology*, 42, 195–206.

Parling, T., Mortazavi, M., & Ghader, A. (2010): Alexithymia and emotional awareness in anorexia nervosa: Time for a shift in the measurement of the concept? *Eating Behaviors*, 11, 205–210.

Pattison, E. M. & Kahan, J. (1983). The deliberate self-harm Syndrome. *American Journal of Psychiatry*, 140, 867–872.

Patton, G. (2012). The natural history of self-harm from adolescence to young adulthood: a population-based cohort study. *Lancet*, 379, 236–243.

Paul, T., Schroeter, K., Dahme, B., & Nutzinger, D. O. (2002). Self-injurious behavior in women with eating disorders. *Self*, 159(3), 408–411.

Pearlman, L. A. (1997). Trauma and the Self: A Theoretical and Clinical Perspective. *Journal of Emotional Abuse*, 1(1), 7–25.

Peterson, J., Feedenthal, S., & Coles, A. (2010). Adolescents who self-harm: How to protect them from themselves. *Current Psychiatry*, 9(8), 15–27.

Plener, P. L., Libal, G., Keller, F., Fegert, J. M., & Muehlenkamp, J. J. (2009). An international comparison of adolescent non-suicidal self-injury (NSSI) and suicide attempts: Germany and the USA. *Psychological Medicine*, 39(9), 1549–58.

Polk, E. & Liss, M. (2007). Psychological characteristics of self-injurious behaviour. *Personality and Individual Differences*, 43, 567–577.

Portzky, G., de Wilde, E., & van Heeringen, K. (2007). Deliberate self-harm in young people: differences in prevalence and risk factors between the Netherlands and Belgium. *European Child & Adolescent Psychiatry*, 17(3), 179186.

Poustie, A. & Neville, R. (2004). Deliberate self harm cases: A primary care perspective. *Nursing Standard*, 18(48), 33–36.

Power, J. & Brown, S. L. (2009). Self-Injurious Behaviour: A Review of the Literature and Implications for Corrections. Ottawa: Correctional Service of Canada. Available from: http://www.csc-scc.gc.ca/005/008/092/ 005008-0216-eng.pdf [Accessed 29 February 2016].

Purington, A. & Whitlock, J. (2010). Non-suicidal self-injury in the media. *The Prevention Researcher*, 17(1), 11–13.

Raudino, A., Fergusson, D. M., & Horwood, L. J. (2013). The quality of parent/child relationships in adolescence is associated with poor adult psychosocial adjustment. *Journal of adolescence*, 36, 331–340.

Regner, J., Burešová, I., Klimusová, H. & Humpolíček, P. (2012). Depresivita jako prediktor výskytu sebepoškozování u dětí [Depression as a predictor of self-harm prevalence in children]. In P. Halama, R. Hanák, R. Masaryk (Eds.),

Sociálne procesy a osobnosť (pp. 128–133). Bratislava: Ústav experimentálnej psychológie SAV.

Renzetti, C. M. & Curran, D. J. (2003). Women, men, and society. London: Allyn and Bacon.

Rheingold, H. (2010). Attention, and Other 21st-Century Social Media Literacies. *EDUCAUSE Review*, 45(5), 14–24.

Richardson, C. (2004). Self-harm: understanding the causes and treatment options. *Nursing Times*, 100(15), 24–25.

Richardson, S. M., Paxron, S. J., & Thomson, J. S. (2009). Is Body Think an efficacious body image and self-esteem program? A controlled evaluation with adolescents. *Body Image*, 2, 75–82.

Rissanen, M. L., Kylmä, J., & Laukkanen, E. (2008). Descriptions of self-mutilation among finnish adolescents: A qualitative descriptive inquiry. *Issues in Mental Health Nursing*, 29, 145–163.

Rogol, A. D., Roemmich, J. N., & Clark, P. A. (2002). Growth at puberty. *Journal of Adolescent Health*, 31, 192–200.

Rosenthal, R. J., Rinzler, C., Wallsh, R., & Klausner, E. (1972). Wrist-cutting syndrome: The meaning of a gesture. *American Journal of Psychiatry*, 128, 47–52.

Ross, R. R. & McKay, H. B. (1979). *Self-Mutilation*. Toronto: Lexington Books.

Ross, S. & Heath, S. (2002). A Study of the Frequency of Self-Mutilation in a Community Sample of Adolescents. *Journal of Youth and Adolescence*, 31(1), 67–77.

Rossotto, E. (1997). *Bulimia nervosa with and without substance use disorders: a comparative study*. Fuller Theological Seminary.

Rossow, I., Ystgaard, M., Hawton, K., Madge, N., Heeringen, K., & Wilde, E., et al. (2007). Cross-national comparisons of the association between alcohol consumption and deliberate self-harm in adolescents. *Suicide & Life – Threatening Behavior*, 37(6), 605–615.

Rowe, S. L., French, R. S., Henderson, C., Ougrin, D., Slade, M. & Moran, P. (2014). Help-seeking behaviour and adolescent self-harm: A systematic review. *Australian and New Zealand Journal of Psychiatry*, 48(12), 1083–1095.

Rozsívalová, E., Trefilová, A., & Paclt, I. (2010). Sebepoškozování u dospívajících [Self-injuring in adolescents]. Česká a slovenská psychiatrie, 106(4), 239–244.

Sabo, A. N., Gunderson, J. G., Najavits L. M., Chauncey, D., & Kisie, C. (1995) Changes in self-destructiveness of borderline patients in psychotherapy. A prospective follow-up. *Journal of Nervous and Mental Disease*, 183, 370–376.

Saçarçelik, G., Türkcan, A., Güveli, H., & Yeşilbaş, D. (2011). The prevalence of deliberace self-harm behavior and its association with sociodemographic features inf patiens referred to secondary care psychiatric clinic for adolescents and young adults. *The Journal of Psychiatry and Neurological Sciences*, 24(4), 253–264.

Sacks, S. R. (2014). Seeking the right fit: From training bras to self-identity as adolescents search for self. In F. R. Spielhagen, P. D. Schwartz (Eds.), *Adolescence in the 21st Century: Constants and Challenges* (pp. 3–22). Charlotte, NC: Information Age Publishing, Inc.

Sansone, R. A. & Levitt, J. L. (2002). Self-harm behaviors among those with eating disorders: An overview. *Eating Disorders*, 10(3), 205–213.

Sansone, R. A. & Sansone, L. A. (2007). Childhood trauma: Borderline personality, and eating disorders: A developmental cascade. *Eating Disorders*, 15, 333–346.

Sansone, R. A. & Sansone, L. A. (2012). Measuring Self-Harm Behavior with the Self-Harm Inventory. *Psychiatry*, 7(4), 16–20.

Sansone, R. A., Sansone, L. A., & Wiederman, M., W. (1995). The prevalence of trauma and its relationship to borderline personality symptoms and self-destructive behaviors in a primary care setting. *Archives of Family Medicine*, 4, 439–442.

Santa Mina, E. E., Gallop, R., Links, P., Heslegrave, R., Pringle, D., Wekerle, C., & Grewal, P. (2006). The Self-Injury Questionnaire: evaluation of the psychometric properties in a clinical population. *Journal of psychiatric and mental health nursing*, 13(2), 221–227.

Scoliers, G., Portzky, G., Madge, N., Hewitt, A., Hawton, K., de Wilde, E. J., et al. (2009). Reasons for adolescent deliberate self-harm: A cry of pain and/or a cry for help? Findings from the Child and Adolescent Self-harm in Europe (CASE) study. *Social Psychiatry and Psychiatric Epidemiology*, 44(8), 601–607.

Selekman, M. D. (2002). Clinical Update: Adolescent Self-harm. *Family Therapy Magazine*, 1(2), 34–39.

Schachter, E. P. & Marschall, S. K. (2008) Agents of identity Formation: A Focus on Those Purposefully Influencing the Identity of Others. *An International Journal of Theory and Research*, 8(2), 183–184.

Schachter, E. P. & Ventura, J. J. (2008). Identity agents: Parents as active and reflective participants in their children's identity formation. *Journal of research on Adolescence*, 18(3), 449–476.

Scharf, M. & Mayseless, O. (2008). Late adolescent girls' relationships with parents and romantic partner: the distinct role of mothers and fathers. *Journal of Adolescence*, 31, 837–855.

Scheirer, L. M. & Hansen, W. B. (2014). *Parenting and Teen Drug Use*. New York: Oxford University Press.

Schulze, U. M., Pettke-Rank, C. V., Kreinkamp, M., Hamm, H., Brocker, E. B., et al. (1999). Dermatologic Findings in Anorexia and Bulimia Nervosa of Childhood and Adolescence. *Pediatric Dermatology*, 16, 90–94.

Simeon, D. & Favazza, A. R. (2001). Self-injurious behaviors: Phenomenology and assessment. In D. Simeon, & E. Hollander (Eds.), *Self-injurious behaviors: Assessment and treatment* (1–28). Washington, DC: American Psychiatric Publishing.

Simon, G. E. (2006). The antidepressant quandary-considering suicide risk when treating adolescent depression. *The New England Journal of Medicine*, 355, 2722–2723.

Simpson, M. A. (1975). The phenomenology of self-mutilation in a general hospital setting. *Canadian Psychiatric Association Journal*, 20, 429–434.

Simpson, M. A. (1980). Self-mutilation as indirect self-destructive behavior. In N. L. Farberow (Ed.), *The many faces of suicide: Indirect self-destructive behavior* (pp. 257–283). New York: McGraw-Hill.

Simpson, C. A. & Porter, G. L. (1981). Self mutilation in children and adolescents. *Bulletin of the Menninger Clinic*, 45, 428–438.

Simpson E., Zlotnick C., & Begin A. (1994). *Self-Injury Survey*. Providence, RI.

Sirotkin, A. V. (2005). Control of reproductive processes by growth hormone: Extra- and intracellular mechanisms. *The Veterinary Journal*, 170, 307–317.

Skegg, K. (2005). Self- harm. *Lancet*, 366, 1471–1483.

Solomon, Y. & Farrand, J. (1996). Why don't you do it properly: Young women who self-injure. *Journal of Adolescence*, 19, 111–119.

Spear, L. (2007). The Developing Brain and Adolescent-Typical Behavior Patterns. An Evolutionary Approach. In D. Romer, E. Walker (Eds.), *Adolescent psychopathology and the developing brain: integrating brain and prevention science*. Oxford: Oxford University Press.

Spender, Q. (2007). Assessment of adolescent self- harm. *Pediatrics and Child Helath*, 17(11), 448–454.

Statham, D. J., Heath, A. C., & Madden, P. A. (1998). Suicidal behaviour: an epidemiological and genetic study. *Psychology and Medicine*, 28, 839–855.

Steensma, T. D., Kreukels, B. P. C., de Vries, A. L. C., & Cohen-Kettenis, P. T. (2013). Gender identity development in adolescence. *Hormones and Behavior*, 64, 288–297.

Steinberg, L. (2005). Cognitive and affective development in adolescence. *Trends in Cognitive Science*, 9(2), 69–75.

St. Germain, S. A & Hooley, J. M (2012). Direct and indirect forms of non-suicidal self-injury: Evidence for a distinction. *Psychiatry Research*, 197, 78–84.

Storey, P., Hurry, J., Jowit, S., Owens, D., & House, A. (2005). Supporting young people who repeatedly self-harm. *Journal of the Royal Society for the Promotion of Health*, 125(2), 71–75.

Sullivan, C., Arensman, E., Keeley, H. S., Corcoran, P., & Perry, I. J. (2004). *Young people's mental health: A report of the results from the Lifestyle and Coping Survey*. Cork, Ireland: National Suicide Foundation.

Sutton, J. (1999). *Healing the Hurt Within: Understand and relieve the suffering behind self-destructive behaviour.* Oxford: How To Books.

Sutton, J. (2005). *Healing the Hurt Within: Understanding Self-injury and Self-harm, and Heal the Emotional Wounds.* 2nd ed. Oxford: How To Books.

Sutton, J. (2007). *Healing the hurt within: Understand self-injury and self-harm, and heal the emotional wounds*. Oxford: How To Content.

Suyemoto, K. L & MacDonald, M. L. (1995). Self-cutting in female adolescents. *Psychotherapy*, 32, 162–171.

Suyemoto, K. L. (1998). The functions of self- mutilation. *Clinical Psychology Review*, 18, 531–554.

Swahn, M. H., Ali, B., Bossarte, R. M., van Dulmen M., Crosby, A., Jones, A. C., & Schinka, K. C. (2012). Self-harm and suicide attempts among high-risk, urban youth in the U. S.: Shared and unique risk and protective factors. *International Journal of Environmental Research and Public Health*, 9(1), 178–191.

Taiminen, T. J., Kallio-Soukainen, K., Nokso-Koivisto, H., Kaljonen, A., & Helenius, H. (1998). Contagion of deliberate self-harm among adolescent inpatients. *Journal of American Academy Child & Adolescent Psychiatry*, 37(2), 211–217.

Tan, A. C. Y., Rehfuss, M. C., Suarez, E. C., & Parks-Savage, A. (2012). Nonsuicidal self-injury in an adolescent population in Singapore. *Clinical Child Psychology and Psychiatry*, 19(1), 58–76.

Tantam, D. & Whittaker, J. (1992). Personality disorder and self wounding. *British Journal of Psychiatry*, 161, 451–464.

Tanti, CH., Stukas, A., A., Halloran, M., J., & Foddy, M. (2011). Social identity change: Shifts in social identity during adolescence. *Journal of Adolescence*, 34, 555–567.

Tick, N. T., van der Ende, J., & Verhulst, F. C. (2008). Ten-year trends in selfreported emotional and behavioral problems of Dutch adolescents. *Social Psychiatry & Psychiatric Epidemiology*, 43(5), 349–355.

Tolmunen, T., Heliste, M., Lehto, S., M., Hintikka, J., Honkalampi, K., & Kauhanen, J. (2011). Stability of Alexithymia in the general population: An 11-year follow-up. *Comprehensive Psychiatry*, 52, 536–541.

Tormoen, A. J., Rossow, I., Larsson, B., & Mehlum, L. (2013). Nonsuicidal self-harm and suicide attempts in adolescents: Differences in kind or in degree? *Social Psychiatry and Psychiatric Epidemiology*, 48(9), 1447–1455.

Townsend, E., Hawton, K., Altman, D. G., Arensman, E., Gunnell, D., et al. (2001). The efficacy of problemsolving treatments after deliberate self-harm: meta-analysis of randomised controlled trials with respect to depression, hopelessness and improvement in problems. *Psychology and Medicine*, 31, 979–88.

Trainor, G. & Wood, A. (2001). Learning to live with life. *Mental Health Care*, 4(8), 273–275.

Transue, L. & Whitlock, J. (2010). Self-injury in the media. [Fact sheet] Cornell Research Program on Self-Injurious Behavior in Adolescents and Young Adults. Available from: http://www.selfinjury.bctr.cornell.edu/documents/media.pdf [Accessed 29 February 2016].

Tuisku, V., Pelkonen, M., Kiviruusu, O., Karlsson, L., Ruuttu, T., & Marttunen, M. (2009). Factors associated with deliberate self-harm behaviour among depressed adolescent outpatients. *Journal of Adolescence*, 32, 1125–1136.

Tyrer, P., Thompson, S., Schmidt, U., Jones, V., Knapp, M., & Davidson, K. et al. (2003). Randomized controlled trial of brief cognitive behaviour therapy versus treatment as usual in recurrent deliberate self-harm: The POMPACT study. *Psychological Medicine*, 33(6), 969–976.

Vaiva, G., Vaiva, G., Ducrocq, F., Meyer, P., Mathieu, D., et al. (2006). Effect of telephone contact on further suicide attempts in patients discharged from an emergency department: Randomised controlled trial. *British medicine Journal*, 332, 1241–5.

Van Camp, I., Desmet, M., & Verhaeghe, P. (2011). Gender differences in non-suicidal self injury: Are they on the verge of levelling off? *International Proceedings of Economics Development & Research*, 23, 28.

Vanderlinden, J. & Vandereycken, W. (1997). *Trauma, dissociation, and impulse dyscontrol in eating disorders*. Philadelphia: Brunner/Mazel.

Vanheule, S. (2008). Challenges for Alexithymia Research: A Commentary on the construct of alexithymia: associations with defense mechanisms. *Journal of Clinical Psychology*, 64(3), 332–337.

Veague, H. B. (2008). *Cutting and Self-harm*. New York: Chelsea House Publishers.

Victor, S. E., Glenn, C. R., & Klonsky, E. D. (2012). Is non-suicidal self-injury an “addiction”? A comparison of craving in substance use and non-suicidal self-injury. *Psychiatry Research*, 197, 73–77.

Viner, R. M., Ozer, E. M., Denny, S., Marmot, M., Resnick, M., Fatusi, A., & Currie, C. (2012). *Adolescence and the social determinants of health*, 379, 1641–1652.

Walsh, B. W. & Rosen, P. (1985). Self-mutilation and contagion: An empirical test. *American Journal of Psychiatry*, 142(1), 119–120.

Walsh, B. W. & Rosen, P. M. (1988). *Self-mutilation: Theory, research and treatment.* New York: Guilford Press.

Wan, Y., Hu, Ch., Hao, J., Sun, Y., & Tao, F. (2011). Deliberate self-harm behaviors in Chinese adolescents and young adults. *European Child & Adolescent Psychiatry*, 20(10), 517–525.

Washburn, J. J., Gebhardt, M., Styer, D. M., Juzwin, K. R., & Gottlieb, L. (2012). Co-occurring disorders in the treatment of nonsuicidal self-injury: An evidence informed approach. *Journal of Cognitive Psychotherapy*, 26(4), 348–364.

Weiss, CH. C. & Baker-Smith, E. CH. (2007). Macrostructural conditions of interpersonal relationships: How schools and schooling shape interactions from early to late adolescence. *Advances in Life Course Research*, 12, 29–54.

Whitlock, J. L. & Selekman, M. (2014). *Non-suicidal self-injury (NSSI) across the lifespan.* In M. Nock (Ed.), Oxford handbook of suicide and self-injury (pp. 133–151). Oxford: Oxford University Press.

Whitlock, J. (2010). What is self-injury? [Fact sheet] Cornell Research Program on Self-Injurious Behavior in Adolescents and Young Adults. Available from: http://www.selfinjury.bctr.cornell.edu/perch/resources/what-is-self-injury-9.pdf [Accessed 29 February 2016].

Wiederman, M. W. & Pryor, T. (1996). Substance use and impulsive behaviors among adolescents with eating disorders. *Addictive Behaviors*, 21(2), 269–272.

Williams, L., Curren, C., & Bruce, G. (2011): Are Alexithymia and type D personality distinct or overlapping constructs? A confirmatory factor analysis of The Toronto Alexithymia and Type D Scales. *Personality and Individual Differences*, 51, 683–686.

Wonderlich, S., Myers, T., Norton, M., & Crosby, R. (2002). Self-harm and bulimia nervosa: A complex connection. *Eating Disorders*, 10, 257–267.

Wong, M. M., Brower, K. J., & Zucker, R. A. (2011). Sleep problems, suicidal ideation, and self-harm behaviors in adolescence. Journal of Psychiatric Research, 45, 505–511.

Wood, A., Trainor, G., Rothwell, J., Moore, A., & Harrington, R. (2001). Randomized trial of group therapy for repeated deliberate self-harm in adolescents. *Journal of the American Academy of Child & Adolescent Psychiatry*, 40(11), 1246–1253.

Yaryua-Tobias, J. A., Neziroglu, F. A., & Kaplan, S. (1995). Self-mutilation, anorexia, and dysmenorrhea in obsessive compulsive disorder. *International Journal of Eating Disorders*, 17, 33–38.

Yates, T. M. (2004). The developmental psychopathology of self-injurious behavior: Compensatory regulation in posttraumatic adaptation. *Clinical Psychological Review*, 24, 35–74.

Ystgaard, M., Arensman, E., Hawton, K., Madge, N., Heeringen, K. V., Hewitt, A., Wilde, E. J. D., De Leo, D., & Fekete, S. (2009). Deliberate self-harm in adolescents: Comparison between those who receive help following self-harm and those who do not. *Journal of Adolescence*, 32, 875–891.

Yusainy, C. & Lawrence, C. (2014). Relating mindfulness and self-control to harm to the self and to others. *Personality and Individual Differences*, 64, 78–83.

Zetterqvist, M., Lundh, L., & Svedin, C. (2012). A comparison of adolescents engaging in self-injurious behaviors with and without suicidal intent: self-reported experiences of adverse life events and trauma symptoms. *Journal of Youth Adolescence*, 42, 1257–1272.

Zimmerman, G., Rossier, J., Meyer de Stadelhofen, F., & Gaillard, F. (2005): Alexithymia Assessment and Relations with Dimensions of Personality. *European Journal of Psychological Assessment*, 21(1), 23–33.

Zlotnick, C., Shea, M. T., Pearlstein, T., Simpson, E., Costello, E., & Being, A. (1996). The relationship between dissociative symptoms, alexithymia, impulsivity, sexual abuse, and self-mutilation. *Comparative Psychiatry*, 37, 12–16.

Zlotnick, C., Wolsdorf, B. A., Johnson, B., & Spirito, A. (2003) Impaired self-regulation and suicidal Behavior among adolescent and young adult psychiatric inpatients. *Archives of Suicide research*, 7, 149–157.

List of Figures

List of Tables

www.ingramcontent.com/pod-product-compliance
Ingram Content Group UK Ltd.
Pitfield, Milton Keynes, MK11 3LW, UK
UKHW020641041026
15590UKWH00001B/20

9 783631 667514